Johnny, aged one

Leon, Nita, Tim, Marion, and Joe, Portugal 1964

Claire at the Leon Pie Fest, 2010

...etra, Jeremy, Mima, and Hattie, 1978

Leon on his ship of the desert, 1959

Jo Jo and Katherine, 1977

Cookbook library at Leon, Old Compton Street

George, 2011

...za, Sadie, Kate, and Joseph, August 1980

Tom Herbert, 1984

Molly, Liza, Emma, Jossy, Kate, Henry, and Anna, 1976

LEON.

Baking & Desserts

BY CLAIRE PTAK & HENRY DIMBLEBY

FOOD PHOTOGRAPHY BY GEORGIA GLYNN SMITH • DESIGN BY ANITA MANGAN

CONTENTS

LEON ENRICHED

Welcome to Leon Baking & Desserts

Leon was founded on the belief that food should taste good and do you good. In this book, we hope to show that this can be the case even where it is often thought impossible—when cooking comfort food. The dishes you will find here look indulgent, sound naughty, and taste like the kind of treats that normally come with a side helping of guilt. Yet, three-quarters of the recipes are wheat, dairy, or sugar free, with plenty of vegan and gluten-free options. You will find an index on page 294 that lets you to look up recipes according to their ingredients:—gluten free, dairy free, and so forth.

The book is divided into two sections. The first part, Every Day, contains recipes for things that you might want to eat throughout the year—breakfast breads, energy bars, cookies and quick desserts. The second part, Celebration, is a collection of recipes designed to celebrate the passing of time, both through the year and through our lives. This is where you will find everything from hot cross buns and toffee apples to a Desperate Dan Pie for Father's Day.

We want this book to be accessible to even the most inexperienced cook—hence our "how-to" sections on basic techniques and tools. Once you have mastered a recipe, you can use our suggested variations to put your own stamp on it. We also want to provide inspiration for the more experienced. Some of the recipes are daring (see Baked Alaska, page 139), some draw on ancient wisdom (see Sourdough Bread, page 196), and some are downright explosive (see Honeycomb Toffee page 220). Each recipe is given a confidence rating—from "beginner" to "feeling brave"—but even the more adventurous recipes shouldn't prove too tricky for the careful amateur.

We hope this book finds a permanent place in your kitchen and becomes batter-splattered, tacky with toffee, and dog-eared through use.

Claire & Henry

A note on the authors

We have written the book in the first person plural—"we"—because it represents the fruits of a year of close collaboration. We are lucky enough to live two doors down from each other, which means we spend a lot of time messing up each other's kitchens and feasting on the results.

But obviously, we bring different things to the party. Simply put, Claire is the professional baker and Henry the enthusiastic amateur.

Claire used to be the pastry chef at Chez Panisse, Alice Waters' legendary restaurant in California. She fell in love with a dapper English DJ and followed him home to east London, where she now runs her acclaimed bakery, Violet. An ardent believer in seasonal, natural ingredients, she is the best baker we know, and there is a precision and delicate beauty to all of her cooking.

Henry is a cofounder of Leon (with John Vincent and Allegra McEvedy). He started his career as a commis chef, but soon realized he was too messy to be a professional cook. He never lost his passion for food, however, and he still spends every spare moment in the kitchen, where he always has some experiment on the go (with his long-suffering wife, Mima, following behind him to clean up). Some of these experiments turn into dishes worth sharing (see Henry's Spiced Chicken Mystery Pie, page 292 and the Chocolate & Salted Caramel Ice Cream Bombe, page 160); others are still being chipped off the ceiling.

There are a few recipes that have appeared in previous Leon books. They have become so popular with our regulars, that we thought it would be wrong to print a book on baking and desserts without them.

Key to Symbols

Key to recipe icons:

♥   Low saturated fats

✓   Good carbs (low GI) / good sugars

WF   Wheat free

GF   Gluten free

DF   Dairy free

V   Vegetarian

🍴   Indulgence

Level of confidence:

Beginner

Medium

Feeling brave

TIPS   Cooking tips, extra information, and alternative ideas.

A lot of lovely people test the recipes to make sure they hit the spot. We've given each one a badge of honor.

GUIDE TO BAKING Ingredients

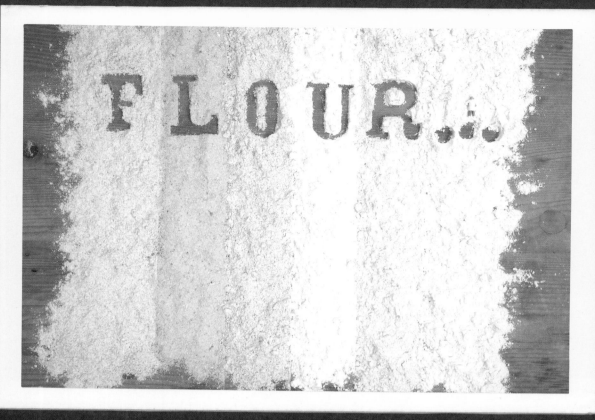

FLOURS, LEFT TO RIGHT: WHOLE-WHEAT SPELT, CORN FLOUR, RYE FLOUR, RICE FLOUR, WHITE SPELT FLOUR & ALL-PURPOSE FLOUR

The role of flours is to provide structure. The proteins in traditional flours react with water, producing gluten, the strands of which create a lattice in which air bubbles can be trapped, giving your baked goods "lightness", but some people find flour hard to digest. Recipes using gluten-free flours will be more cakelike, although this effect can often be offset to some degree by adding other structure providers, such as eggs or gums.

① TRADITIONAL WHEAT FLOUR

Whole-wheat, all-purpose/white bread, and self-rising

What is it? Ground wheat. Whole-wheat is made from the whole grain: the endosperm (proteinous/starchy), the germ (proteinous and full of vitamins), and the bran (fibrous). The other varieties of wheat are made from the starchy endosperm only. All-purpose white flour is used for general baking as it produces less gluten than strong flour, which is traditionally used to make bread. Self-rising flour is all-purpose flour with a leavening agent (such as baking powder) added, plus salt.

What is it good for? Pretty much anything in traditional baking.

Is it good for me? For a lot of people, no. Wheat has changed beyond recognition in the past 100 years, as farmers have selectively bred it from its naturally occurring forms to the extremely high-yielding grains that are produced today. These advances have done a lot to help feed a growing global population, but at a cost. Incidences of celiac disease—a severe allergy to gluten, that causes the immune system to attack the lining of the small intestine—have been doubling every fifteen years since the 1970s. Some people are also allergic to wheat (rather than just to the gluten it contains). In addition wheat intolerance is a growing problem—a less catastrophic but still unpleasant reaction to modern wheat proteins that can leave you feeling heavy, tired, and listless. If you are lucky enough to have a body that can cope with it, wheat is a wonderful thing. If not, there are alternatives.

② SPELT FLOUR
Whole grain or fine

What is it? Spelt is an ancient variety of wheat that has not been transformed by selective breeding.

What is it good for? You can use spelt as a substitute for wheat in many dishes. Although it is higher in protein than many wheat flours, it is lower in gluten. It will not, therefore, give you the extravagantly risen breads that you can create with wheat flour. It has a delicious nutty flavor. We love spelt.

Is it good for you? People with wheat allergy and intolerance can generally tuck into spelt quite happily. Celiacs must avoid spelt because it contains gluten. Our own experience is that it doesn't give you that bloated sensation you get from traditional wheat.

③ RYE FLOUR

What is it? Rye comes from the same family of grasses as wheat. It originated in Eastern Europe, where it grows well in cold climates and in poor soil. It is dense and dark and contains little gluten.

What is it good for? For making traditional rye breads (see page 201). Also strongly flavored beers, vodka, and whiskey.

Is it good for you? Many people find it more palatable than wheat, because it has lower gluten levels and has been less intensively bred. It is high in vitamins and soluble fiber, and has a lower glycemic load than many wheat and spelt breads, so is less likely to lead to weight gain.

④ BUCKWHEAT FLOUR

What is it? Buckwheat is actually not a wheat at all. It is not even a grass. It is a fruit seed from the rhubarb family and similar to a sunflower seed. It is gluten free.

What is it good for? We use the flour to make pancakes, the flakes to make granola and oatmeal, and it can be used as a couscous substitute in its groat form. However, it will not provide sufficient structure to make breads unless you add eggs or xanthan gum. It can also be used alongside other flours for interesting flavor and texture combinations.

Is it good for you? Yes. It is high in nutrients, especially manganese and magnesium, and also provides vitamins, zinc, and a whole host of other goodies. It is sometimes called the "king of the healing grains".

5 GLUTEN-FREE FLOUR

What is it? Any flour that does not contain gluten. You can mix your own or choose storebought types, which will generally be various blends of rice, potato, buckwheat, and bean and pea flours. They will often have added gluten substitutes, such as xantham gum.

What is it good for? If you want to avoid gluten, you can use it as a flour substitute in instances where the dish you are making does not need the strong structure that gluten provides. In this book, we use it in crumbles, scones, cakes, tarts, and to make a "cakey" breakfast loaf.

Is it good for you? These flours will not contain gluten, but some are quite refined so they will not necessarily be packed full of nutrients.

6 CORNMEAL

What is it? Coarsely ground dried corn/maize, also known as polenta. As opposed to cornstarch, which is very finely ground into a starchy white powder.

What is it good for? We use it to give body to cakes while avoiding wheat flour. It has a beautiful yellow color and a mild, sweet flavor.

Is it good for you? It a relatively complex carbohydrate that also contains protein and some vitamins. A reasonable food— it won't make a superhero of you overnight, but it isn't bad for you either.

7 CHICKPEA (BESAN) FLOUR

What is it? Ground-up dried chickpeas.
What is it good for? We use it to add body to some gluten-free cakes. Also good for thickening stews. It can be a little bitter, so we like to use it sparingly.
Is it good for you? Yes. Gluten free, it has a low GL, so it won't set your sugar levels racing. Contains a good bit of protein and iron.

LEAVENERS & THICKENERS

1 YEAST
A microorganism that converts the sugars in flour into carbon dioxide bubbles, thus putting air into the dough. It comes in many forms— fresh, dry, and active dry. We specify the type used in each recipe, but if you are substituting one for another, make sure you follow the instructions on the package.

2 BAKING SODA
A chemical compound with a slightly alkaline taste, which reacts with acids to form carbon dioxide.

3 BAKING POWDER
A mixture of baking soda and an acid compound (typically cream of tartar) that reacts when moistened to produce carbon dioxide. (Some baking powders use wheat as a "moisture absorption agent". You can buy gluten-free ones that do not.)

4 ARROWROOT, CORNSTARCH
Starchy powders useful for gluten-free binding and thickening.

5 XANTHUM GUM
A thickener/binder that can be used at very low concentrations to thicken sauces. Often used to help give gluten-free breads structure.

6 EGG SUBSTITUTE
Also known as whole egg replacer, it is used to replace eggs in sponges and cakes for vegans and people who are allergic. Normally made of soy protein and potato starch. Not something we use often, but nice if you are baking for a vegan.

FATS

Fats play many roles in baking. They add moistness and tenderness. They create barriers between layers of flour, allowing crispy pastries to develop. They help gluten stretch in bread, and are used to stop things sticking to baking sheets. They taste rich and sweet.

❶ UNSALTED BUTTER

What is it? A golden block of dairy goodness made from churning cream to concentrate the butterfat. It is an emulsion of butterfat (about 80%), water, and milk proteins. Unsalted butter is normally used in baking, because it has a sweeter flavour.

What is it good for? The most common baking fat, butter is solid at room temperature and can, therefore, be used to make all kinds of flaky pastries. It melts at body temperature, so it doesn't taste greasy.

Is it good for me? As with suet (see page 18), butter is mostly saturated fat and is, therefore, high in calories. These foods used to be considered the devil's work, but they are all natural and recent nutritional research suggests that (within reason) they are likely to do us less harm than processed alternatives. Because it is a saturated fat, butter can also be heated without changing its structure and becoming more harmful. Butter contains very little lactose and is, therefore, less of a problem for the lactose intolerant.

❷ SALTED BUTTER

What is it? Butter that has had salt added as a preservative and to change the flavor.

What is it good for? Generally, we prefer the sweeter flavor of unsalted butter in baking and desserts. But occasionally—for example the Sweet Popcorn with Chocolate Drizzle, see page 79—the stronger flavor of salted butter gets the nod.

Is it good for me? Much the same as unsalted butter. If you need to watch your salt levels, then go for unsalted.

❸ COCONUT OIL

What is it? The oil extracted from coconut flesh.

What is it good for? It is liquid at body temperature, but just about solid at room temperature. This makes it a possible substitute for butter in many applications (although, as you will see from the recipes, you have to handle it differently). Its melting point (about 73°F) is much closer to room temperature than butter (about 90°F) or indeed cocoa butter (about 94°F) which gives it unique qualities. Coconut oil frosting (see page 97) for example, melts in the mouth in a very different way from the richer buttercreams. (If you have ever tried Lindt Lindor chocolates—which contain a lot of coconut oil—you will recognize the sensation.)

Is it good for me? There is a great deal of debate over this. When people started trying to cut dairy out of their diet, coconut oil was seen as a perfect substitute. Then nutritionists pointed out that it was also high in calories and saturated fats. More recent evidence has shown that coconut oil actually promotes good cholesterol and that it is easily metabolized into fuel (rather than deposited as fat). Of course, this is only useful if you need the fuel. Our feeling is that it is a good fat; some people say it will make you podgy, but many nutritionists disagree. Claire ate loads of it on a recent detox and the weight fell off. (Read labels carefully however, because some coconut oil is still hydrogenated, which is bad news. Always choose organic and unrefined).

④ OLIVE OIL

What is it? Cold-pressed extra virgin olive oil is the oil extracted from olive flesh.
What is it good for? It is liquid at room temperature and, therefore, less versatile in baking than other fats discussed here. We use it in breads and pizza doughs and to toast granola.
Is it good for you? Yes. It is high in monounsaturated fats that may help protect against heart disease. It also contains a useful source of omega-6 fats, which we must eat because our bodies cannot make them from other foods. (Make sure you get the cold-pressed variety.)

⑤ SUET

What is it? Raw beef (and sometimes mutton) fat, often taken from around the kidneys. The stuff that you buy from the butchers has been dehydrated, purified, and mixed with flour to stabilize it. If you use real fresh suet, you may need slightly less. (You can also buy vegetarian suet, but choose carefully: most of it is made from hydrogenated trans-fats, which should be avoided.)
What is it good for? Making traditional steamed English puddings. The suet is hard and, therefore, forms little pockets in the pastry. When the pudding is cooking, these melt away, leaving air pockets and giving that wonderful light, spongy, and slightly crispy texture. If you substitute butter, you will get a much denser, richer pastry.
Is it good for me? It is a high-calorie saturated fat. However, the link between saturated fat and heart disease is now under dispute, with recent studies pointing to manufactured trans-fats and sugary foods as the real villains. Therefore: Don't eat suet every day, but it's fine as an occasional treat.

⑥ LARD

What is it? Pig fat—often rendered (melted slowly), purified and then reset.
What is it good for? Generally, used to make really flaky pastries (for example, the hot crust pastry used for the pork pie on page 284). It is solid at body temperature and has a distinct soft porky flavor. We don't use it much.
Is it good for you? Very calorific, but probably not as sinful as its reputation would suggest. Eat it about as often as you would suet (see left).

⑦ MARGARINE

What is it? A butter substitute originally manufactured from beef fat but now more commonly made by thickening vegetable oils and dying them yellow.
What is it good for? Absolutely nothing. Say it again. We don't think that there is any recipe that tastes better when made with margarine.
Is it good for you? Traditional margarines made from hydrogenating vegetable oil were originally marketed as a healthier, cheaper alternative to butter. We now know that the manufacturing process created deadly trans-fats, and these types of marg have all but disappeared from the supermarket shelves. More recent manufacturing methods have produced a slew of margarines with their own advertised "health benefits". However, they have only recently entered the food chain and we would council caution. Our general rule of thumb is: Avoid using any ingredient in cooking that has been invented in the last 1,000 years.

SUGARS & SWEETENERS

It is one of the tragedies of the human condition that sweet foods were not that commonplace when our palates were evolving. To early man, sugar was a rare and valuable source of energy. As a result, we have evolved to seek it out and wolf it down. Our taste buds, which usually guide us toward things that are good for us, tell us that sweet things are to be gobbled up with abandon.

Until as recently as 1766, when the Sugar Tax was repealed, it was impossible to get hold of sugar in sufficient quantity to do us harm. White processed sugar is now cheap and plentiful, and over the last couple of decades it has been recognized (alongside processed carbohydrates) as the single greatest threat to our health. In the end, moderation is the answer, but there are some sweet substances out there that enable us to satisfy those evolutionary instincts while offering a little more protection to our bodies.

SUGAR

Sugar is made by distilling a sweet syrup—usually taken from sugar cane or sugar beet—until it crystallizes. It is almost irresistible. We try to use substitutes where possible. Where you do use it, here are a few rules:

Use cane sugar not beet sugar. Beet sugar has a funny taste, particularly noticeable in icings and frostings.

Use unrefined sugar—it has a slightly nicer taste and at least retains some minerals and nutrients.

Eat as only a treat. Otherwise it will make your blood sugar soar and then slump, leaving you a bit moody and, later, a bit fatter.

Sugar comes in many forms from a superfine * variety to a dark brown Barbados type. If you are ever on vacation in a sugar-producing country, take an afternoon to visit a sugar refinery. They are amazing places. The cane is ground by vast grooved metal rollers sprayed with hot water, and the resulting syrup is boiled to varying levels of darkness in bubbling vats. The smell is intoxicating. Unrefined sugars are spun off from the syrups at varying levels of concentration (each darker than the last), using a centrifuge. The final remaining sweet syrup is called molasses, which is dense in nutrients compared to other sugars.

The sugars we use are:

1 UNREFINED SUPERFINE SUGAR

Unrefined means it contains molasses; refined sugar has this source of nutrients and flavor removed. Unrefined cane sugar comes from an early stage of distillation, and the brown of the molasses is hardly visible. The crystals are ground, which makes them easy to mix, melt, and dissolve.

2 UNREFINED DEMERARA SUGAR

Darker than superfine sugar, this is a raw sugar with a stronger flavor. Larger crystals give it a satisfyingly crunchy bite.

3 DARK BROWN BARBADOS SUGAR

This sugar (also called muscovado sugar) is not spun in the centrifuge, but is left to dry in the sun. It, therefore, contains more plant matter, which gives it its rich flavor. It is very different from, and much nicer than, the brown sugar made by adding molasses to white sugar.

4 CONFECTIONERS' SUGAR

A finely ground sugar, it often contains an anti-caking agent.

5 MOLASSES

The syrup left over when the sugar crystals have been spun out. Light molasses is made from the by-product of the first white sugar production. Dark molasses is made from later boilings and contains more plant matter and less sugar (about 55 percent sugar).

6 FRUCTOSE

The sugar in cane sugar is sucrose, which is made up of glucose and fructose (the latter also occurs naturally in fruit). Sugar can be treated to create fructose, which we use in our brownies because it's less likely to give you a sugar high followed by a sugar low and is, therefore, good for afternoon concentration. However, there is recent evidence to suggest that it might turn to fat more easily than other sugars. In this book we, therefore, use a number of other natural sweeteners.

Natural sweeteners are generally used because they cause less of a sugar rush than traditional sugar and are less refined—therefore, containing more nutrients. However, they still come with some caveats.

7 HONEY

Flower nectar collected by bees.
What is good about it? Completely natural and delicious. Many forms are high in fructose and, therefore, create less of a sugar rush.
Any problems? Much mass-market honey is made by feeding the bees sugar syrup—and so is nutritionally identical to sugar.

8 MAPLE SYRUP

A syrup from the sap of maple trees.
What is good about it? Like honey, it is natural and delicious.
Any problems? The sweetness in maple syrup comes mostly from sucrose, and, therefore, it carries the same health warnings as sugar.

9 AGAVE NECTAR

A syrup produced from the Mexican agave plant. It is sweeter than honey, but less viscous.
What is good about it? It tastes good and is much less likely to give you a sugar rush.
Any problems? Due to massive recent demand, much of it is now quite heavily processed. Fructose is its main source of sweetness, and fructose may not be as innocent as once thought. Agave nectar's reputation as a miracle substitute for sugar has suffered as a result.

10 BROWN RICE SYRUP

This is derived by culturing cooked rice with enzymes from dried barley sprouts to break down the starches, which is then strained off and the resulting sweet liquid cooked.
What is good about it? It is a natural product that will not give you a sugar rush and does not contain fructose.
Any problems? It is pretty strongly flavored. It has not been widely available for long, but so far seems to have a clean bill of health.

11 YACON SYRUP

A dark molasses-like syrup made from a Peruvian root.
What is good about it? Unlike agave syrup, the compounds providing the sweetness in yacon syrup pass through the body without being metabolized at all.
Any problems? It has a pretty strong flavor. As yet, no one has claimed that it is bad for you.

12 STEVIA

A mintlike herb that is very sweet but contains no calories. Recently hailed as the potential solution to the sugar problem.
What is good about it? Sweet without an aftertaste and contains no calories. Will not give you a sugar rush.
Any problems? It is almost impossible to get hold of unless you grow it in your own garden. No detailed research has been carried out on possible side effects. There is a heated ongoing controversy over whether sweetener companies are exerting political power to prevent it from coming to market. In the US it is available if labeled as a dietary supplement or as a food additive.

OTHER BITS & PIECES

SPIRULINA

RICE MILK

BRAZIL NUTS

SHELLED HEMP SEEDS

TAHINI

AGAR FLAKES

OAT BRAN

AGAVE NECTAR

CASHEW NUTS

COCONUT BUTTER

YACAN SYRUP

CHIA SEED

BROWN RICE SYRUP

TOOLS, TIPS & TECHNIQUES

TOOLS

If you are new to baking, the sheer number of available tools and gadgets can be unnerving (and expensive if you find shiny new toys hard to resist). Here are the ones that we use most.

BASIC TOOLS

1 ROLLING PIN

We like a nice long one. Most materials are fine, but wood is nice and light—just make sure the grain is fine or it will leave marks on your dough. You don't need handles; in fact, you can get a better feel by rolling your palms over the top of the pin.

2 WHISK

For breaking up eggs, sifting flour (if it does not need to be super-fine), creaming softened butter, and breaking up granita. A silicon whisk is good if you are using it in a non stick pan (although they are not as long-lasting).

3 STRAINER

Good to have a couple of different sizes—a small one for dusting and a bigger one for sifting. The more sturdy ones with the metal rim will withstand a good bash when you are sifting. (They are beautiful things, sieves, if you look at them closely.)

4 SPATULA (OR LAST LICK)

For making sure that you get everything out of the bowl, even if the last bits are just going straight into your mouth. Great for folding things together (such as chocolate and whisked egg whites). The heatproof ones are useful for stirring custard.

5 HANDHELD ELECTRIC MIXER

It's all well and good being macho and using a standard whisk when people are about, but when you are on your own an electric one is so much easier. For creaming butter and sugar, making meringues, and so forth.

6 PARCHMENT PAPER

Please don't try to use a thin wax paper in place of proper parchment paper. Parchment makes life much easier—whether you are lining cake pans or pouring hot cracknel onto it, it will not let you down by breaking up into tiny pieces.

7 MICROPLANE ZESTER

For getting the zest off citrus fruits. If you are using a traditional zester, you will need to chop it finely. Make sure you aren't so seduced by the microplane's easy action that you absentmindedly shred the white pith into your cake—it is very bitter. These are also great for grating Parmesan.

8 ICE CREAM SCOOP

Use the traditional kind to make sure that your ice cream balls are beautifully proportioned. The quick-release ones are useful for portioning things—such as cupcakes—but are often not strong enough for the hardness of ice cream from modern freezers.

9 MEASURING SPOONS

Have one standard kitchen set and use them for everything. Whether this is superstition or not, we find that different sets seem to vary slightly. It is safer and your baking will be more consistent if you just get used to one.

10 LIQUID MEASURING CUP

Great as a general receptacle for tidy baking. Use the measuring cup to portion runny batter out into prepared baking pans, for example. To accurately measure liquids, always put the measuring cup on a level surface and look at the liquid at eye level.

11 SPEED PEELER

Owning any other kind of peeler is a form of madness—a little like when Björn Borg tried to make his comeback in professional tennis using a wooden racket. The speed peelers are by far the most effective.

12 PARING KNIFE

For all those little jobs, such as freeing cakes from pans, trimming fruits, or scoring bread dough.

13 JUICER (OR REAMER)

Great for getting all the juice out of a small amount of fruit. Cheap, easy to clean, efficient, durable, beautiful, simple, and safe.

14 SCALES & MEASURING CUPS

Electric scales, available from specialty baking suppliers, are brilliant for home bakers, because they are so precise. A set of measuring cups is also essential. They come in ¼ cup, ⅓ cup, ½ cup and 1 cup sizes.

15 BAKING PANS

The basics:
- Two 8½-inch loaf pans.
- A deep muffin tin (and maybe a mini muffin pan).
- Two 8–9 inch cake pans (round, with approximately 1-inch-deep edges)—with a push-out removeable bottom if possible.
- An 8–9 inch tart pan with fluted edges (approximately 1-inch-deep) with a push-out removeable bottom if possible.
- A deep cake pan for fruitcakes, again with a removeable bottom (and maybe a springform cake pan for cheesecakes).

(See our pull-out baking pan guide between pages 32 and 33.)

A BAKER WE LOVE

ELISABETH PTAK

Cakes and candies were a big part of my mother Elisabeth's childhood. The photograph of her on her fourth birthday (above) tells the story. Her brothers and friends are gathered around the table, where the birthday girl (Mom) has the task of blowing out the candles on *three* birthday cakes.

Usually, her mother (my grandmother) or her aunt was in charge of the baking duties but as soon as she was old enough, Mom happily became the family cake-maker, and passed that love on to me and my brother (who quickly established a reputation for some of the best chocolate chip cookies around).

Mom always lays a beautiful table and has a party whenever she can. She tends to make not one but four or five different desserts, so that there is a lot of choice.

Her Lemon Bars (see page 94) are legendary.

CLAIRE

ADVANCED TOOLS

1 IMMERSION BLENDER
For making fruit purees, seed milks, bringing chocolate and butter mixes back if they have split, and mixing flavors, such as green peppercorns into the Green Peppercorn Ice Cream recipe on page 250. (Also great for soups and smoothies.)

2 FREESTANDING MIXER
If you do a lot of baking, this will save you a great deal of time and mess.

3 DOUGH SCRAPER
For cutting bread dough, and scraping it (and loose flour) off surfaces. Also useful for folding (such as egg white into melted chocolate).

4 ICE CREAM MACHINE
A complete luxury, because you can make great ice cream without one (see pages 150–161). On the other hand, you could have a lot of fun with it and it saves time.

5 FROSTING SPATULA
For frosting, leveling cake mixes, and lifting delicate cakes and cookies onto cooling racks. Good to have a couple of sizes.

6 BIRD'S BEAK
A speciality paring knife for trimming fruit into particularly pleasing shapes (such as for coring the apples in Tarte Tatin on page 116.)

7 ZESTER
For when you need a hit of zesty flavor and you are going to strain out the zest, for example in a poaching liquid or ice cream base. You can also make delicate strands of candied zest by poaching them in a simple syrup.

8 LARGE METAL WHISK
If you are planning to get serious about your baking—either baking in large quantities, or baking for the long term—these professional whisks will offer unflagging support.

TECHNIQUES

Although all the recipes in this book contain enough instructions for you to plunge straight in, what follows is intended as a kind of mini masterclass in baking techniques. The first two sections—Basic Techniques and Advanced Techniques—give a brief run-through for the relatively inexperienced or rusty baker. (Even the more experienced may find they pick up a thing or two along the way.)

The third section—Baking with Alternatives—is a primer on the changes you will need to make to your baking style if you are cooking without that traditional triumvirate of baking ingredients: flour, butter, and/or sugar. Many of the recipes in this book are wheat, dairy, or sugar free, and this section will get your confidence up before you attempt them. You can also use these guidelines to help you transform your own traditional recipes into healthier ones.

BASIC TECHNIQUES

① GENERAL TIPS

Make notes
You never know when you will try an experiment that creates something wonderful. Get into the habit of having a pencil and paper on hand to jot down what you have done.

If you are substituting ingredients, be prepared to experiment
For example, if you use spelt flour in place of whole-wheat flour, or fructose instead of sugar, you will find that their properties are different. They will produce different textures, absorb different amounts of liquid, and so on. Don't let this put you off

experimentation—just be aware of it and observe the results in case you want to tweak the recipes next time.

Measure everything out first
Chefs call this "mise en place"—literally, "put in place". It makes the whole process more ordered and enjoyable. If you are a man, there is a chance that you will forget this advice.

> MAKE SURE YOU HAVE THE RIGHT SIZE PAN OR DISH IN ADVANCE FOR THE RECIPE YOU ARE MAKING.

② MIXING & MEASURING

Weigh ingredients on kitchen scales
Many professional bakers prefer to use scales because they are more accurate at measuring large quantities of dry ingredients. For similar results, always use standard standard kitchen measuring cups. Use the back of a knife blade to level the ingredients in a cup.

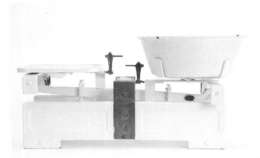

CONVERSION CHART FOR COMMON MEASURES

MEASUREMENTS

5 mm	$1/4$ inch
1 cm	$1/2$ inch
1.5 cm	$3/4$ inch
2.5 cm	1 inch
5 cm	2 inches
7 cm	3 inches
10 cm	4 inches
12 cm	5 inches
15 cm	6 inches
18 cm	7 inches
20 cm	8 inches
23 cm	9 inches
25 cm	10 inches
28 cm	11 inches
30 cm	12 inches
33 cm	13 inches

OVEN TEMPERATURES

110°C	(225°F)	Gas Mark $1/4$
120°C	(250°F)	Gas Mark $1/2$
140°C	(275°F)	Gas Mark 1
150°C	(300°F)	Gas Mark 2
160°C	(325°F)	Gas Mark 3
180°C	(350°F)	Gas Mark 4
190°C	(375°F)	Gas Mark 5
200°C	(400°F)	Gas Mark 6
220°C	(425°F)	Gas Mark 7
230°C	(450°F)	Gas Mark 8

LIQUIDS

15 ml	$1/2$ fl oz
25 ml	1 fl oz
50 ml	2 fl oz
75 ml	3 fl oz
100ml	$3 1/2$ fl oz
125 ml	4 fl oz
150 ml	$1/4$ pint
175 ml	6 fl oz
200 ml	7 fl oz
250 ml	8 fl oz
275 ml	9 fl oz
300 ml	$1/2$ pint
325 ml	11 fl oz
350 ml	12 fl oz
375 ml	13 fl oz
400 ml	14 fl oz
450 ml	$3/4$ pint
475 ml	16 fl oz
500 ml	17 fl oz
575 ml	18 fl oz
600 ml	1 pint
750 ml	$1 1/4$ pints
900 ml	$1 1/2$ pints
1 litre	$1 3/4$ pints
1.2 litres	2 pints
1.5 litres	$2 1/2$ pints
1.8 litres	3 pints
2 litres	$3 1/2$ pints
2.5 litres	4 pints
3.6 litres	6 pints

WEIGHTS

5 g	$1/4$ oz
15 g	$1/2$ oz
20 g	$3/4$ oz
25 g	1 oz
50 g	2 oz
75 g	3 oz
125 g	4 oz
150 g	5 oz
175 g	6 oz
200 g	7 oz
250 g	8 oz
275 g	9 oz
300 g	10 oz
325 g	11 oz
375 g	12 oz
400 g	13 oz
425 g	14 oz
475 g	15 oz
500 g	1 lb
625 g	$1 1/4$ lb
750 g	$1 1/2$ lb
875 g	$1 3/4$ lb
1 kg	2 lb
1.25 kg	$2 1/2$ lb
1.5 kg	3 lb
1.75 kg	$3 1/2$ lb
2 kg	4 lb

Working with different types of oven

All the recipes in this book have been tested in an oven without a fan.
If you are using this kind of oven, you should put the cake in the middle of the
middle shelf, because heat rises and the top can be hotter than the bottom.

If you are using a fan-assisted oven, lower the temperature given in the recipe
by 20°C. Modern fan-assisted ovens are very efficient at circulating heat evenly
around the oven, so there's also no need to worry about positioning. Even if
you have a few racks filled, the heat will be pushed by the fan all around the
baking cakes.

Regardless of what type of oven you use you will find that it has its
idiosyncrasies, so don't stick slavishly to any baking recipes. Make sure you
understand how your oven behaves and adjust accordingly.

A GUIDE TO
Baking Dishes

Muffin tin

Spring-form tin

Square cake tin

Deep cake tin

Loaf tin

Baking sheet

Loose-bottomed tin

Small pie dish

Saucepan

Roasting tray

Ramekin

American pie dish

Flan dish /
American tart dish

Griddle pan

Deep baking dish / tray

Sifting with a strainer

Put the ingredients that you want to sift into a strainer held over a bowl. Tip the strainer to an angle of 30 degrees and knock the lower edge with a metal spoon or the back of a knife until everything has passed through. With confectioners' sugar, you can crush the last few balls through with the back of a spoon.

Combining dry ingredients

Sometimes sifting is not necessary. If you don't mind lumps, and are only trying to evenly distribute leavening agents or spices through a large quantity of flour, using a handheld whisk is a great shortcut.

Creaming

There are two ways to cream your butter and sugar. The recipes in this book will each say which one to use.

Traditional: This method is slightly more painstaking, but gives the lightest cakes. You mix the butter (softened) vigorously with the sugar (ideally with an electric mixer) to trap air. You then mix in the other ingredients gradually in the following order – eggs, then some flour, then some liquid, then the rest of the flour, then the rest of the liquid.

The two-stage mixing method: More common in this country, it produces soft but slightly heavier cakes. It is quicker. You mix all the dry ingredients in one bowl, then mix the butter into those (as if making pastry) before adding the wet ingredients until incorporated.

Folding

This is how you mix two semiliquid substances while preserving the air trapped in one of them (for example, melted chocolate and whisked egg, or fruit puree and whipped cream). We were taught slightly different ways to fold, but the principle remains the same: Do it gently and without any obviously "crushing" or "deflating" motions.

Claire's method: Use a rubber spatula to gently but quickly fold together aerated eggs or cream with other ingredients. Swirls will form in the mixture but don't worry about mixing until they are gone, because you run the risk of overmixing.

Henry's method: Put the mixture with the air in it on top of the other mixture in a large bowl. Take a large metal spoon and cut vertically down into the middle of the bowl. When you hit the bottom, scoop the spoon around toward you, gently lifting the mixture and folding it back on top of the bowl. Rotate the bowl by 45 degrees and repeat until mixed.

Buying eggs
Choose a decent-size, free-range egg. Chickens that have been well fed and cared for produce yolks that are more yellow and lustrous. The yellow or orange yolks can be indicative of the seasons, because the greener the grass that the chickens are eating, the deeper the color of the yolks.

Bringing eggs to temperature
When using eggs for baking, they should ideally be at room temperature. If you are getting them straight from the refrigerator, you can plunge them into warm water for a couple of minutes to speed up the process.

Quick Custard

Makes: 2½ cups
Preparation time: 5 minutes
Cooking time: 15 minutes
WF GF V

1 **vanilla bean**
2 cups **double cream**
½ cup **milk**
1 cup **superfine sugar**
5 **free-range egg yolks**, at room temperature
sea salt

1. Halve the vanilla bean lengthwise and put it into a saucepan with the cream, milk, and superfine sugar. Bring to a boil, stirring to make sure the sugar dissolves. Remove the pan from the heat and let it sit for 5 minutes.

2. Meanwhile, put your egg yolks into a blender and blend for 2 minutes, or until they turn creamy. Add a small pinch of salt.

3. Bring the cream back to a boil, remove the vanilla bean, and pour the mixture slowly into the eggs, blending as you work. Assuming that the cream was good and hot and the eggs not too cold, you should be left with great not-too-thick custard. (If you want to make it thicker, heat it gently on the stove, but you shouldn't need to.)

 TIPS

❧ By using more cream than in most recipes, and—critically—heating the sugar with the cream, instead of adding it to the egg yolks, you remove the nervous stage of heating the custard over the stove and waiting for it to thicken—or, more often than not, scramble.

Breaking eggs

Break the shells against a flat counter, instead of against the edge of the bowl or with a knife or spoon. This way, pieces of shell are less likely to get forced into the egg.

Separating eggs

Holding the two halves of the broken egg above a bowl, plop the yolk from one half shell to the other, back and forth, until all the white has fallen into the bowl. Then drop the yolk into another, smaller bowl. (If the yolk starts to break up, move fast and get the yolk into the yolks bowl. It is better to have a little white in the yolks bowl than a little yolk in the whites bowl. Yolk contamination makes it harder to whisk the whites, see below.)

Beating egg whites

This is one of the few cases where fresher is not better. It is actually slightly easier to whisk the whites of older, runnier eggs. (The whites of a fresh egg will be very coagulated.) MAKE SURE THE BOWL AND THE BEATERS OR WHISK ARE VERY CLEAN. A little dirt—particularly fat, which you find in egg yolks—can prevent a good voluminous cloud of whites (although a speck of yolk won't matter). A pinch of salt or cream of tartar helps the beating. Be careful not to overbeat egg whites; once they have formed stiff peaks, beating them further will cause them to granulate and break down.

④ CHOCOLATE—BASIC
(see also page 44)

Buying

Most of the recipes here call for a high cocoa solid chocolate (over 70 percent). With chocolate you generally get what you pay for. There are, however, many single-origin chocolates available these days that can be as low as 64 percent and still have very good characteristics and flavour. They are usually pretty expensive, but they're a nice treat.

Storing

Heat and water are the enemies of chocolate. A damp climate draws the sugar out and produces that white coating on the surface called bloom. Bloom does not affect the taste of chocolate; it just looks bad. If chocolate melts slightly and resets, it can lose the "temper" which gives it its lovely finish and that satisfying "snap" when you break it. It will keep for ages somewhere airtight and coolish (but not in the refrigerator, which tends to be damp and, therefore encourages bloom).

Melting

As we say above, chocolate hates heat. It will melt at a temperature of 93°F, just under body temperature (which is why it literally melts in the mouth so deliciously). If you heat it over 122°F, the emulsifiers become damaged and it starts to split into its constituent parts—fats and solids. So heat it carefully in a saucepan suspended over another saucepan containing very gently simmering water. (Be careful not to get any drops of water into the melting chocolate, because these can cause hard lumps to form.) You can melt large quantities of chocolate in an accurate oven set at under 122°F – this may take a couple of hours. It is possible to melt chocolate in a saucepan over gentle heat, stirring consistently, but it's not advised. You can also use a microwave to melt the chocolate in 30-second blasts, stirring in between the blasts.

5 CREAM

Types of cream
Creams are named according to the amount of fat they contain. Broadly speaking, creams with a higher fat percentage will be richer and thicker, and easier to whip. The higher fat content creams are also more stable, and, therefore, less prone to curdling when heated or when acid is added to them. For example, a heavy cream (which is high in fat) can be boiled, whereas a light cream might split under the same treatment. Likewise, you can squeeze lemon juice into heavy cream with abandon, but you might want to be careful with light cream.

The names of creams varies by country. In this country the main types are:

Light cream
Contains no less than 18 percent fat, and normally around 20 percent. It splits easily, so is generally used cold in coffee or as table cream. It won't whip up, no matter how hard you go at it.

Sour cream
A cream with 18 to 20 percent fat that has been soured by adding lactic acid. It has a distinctive tang. As well as being used in some baking recipes, it is often used as a condiment where richness and sharpness are sought (for example, in dips, to top baked potatoes, or in burritos).

Heavy cream
Also called heavy whipping cream it contains 36 percent fat. Light whipping cream, with 30 to 36 percent fat also available, will whip very readily and does not curdle. It is easy to overwhip it and set it far too hard.

Crème fraîche
A naturally thickened unpasturized cream of French origin. Here, pasturized cream is fermented with either sour cream or buttermilk to produce a suitable substitute. It has a lovely tang to it. Good for spooning on desserts or using in sauces. Doesn't split easily.

Clotted cream
A high-fat cream popular in England that has been slowly heated and cooled until thickly set. Look for it in specialty stores. Contains over 55 percent fat. For spooning on desserts (clotted cream scooped onto ice cream is a rare summer treat). Don't heat it, because it will melt and split like butter.

Half-and-half
Equal amounts of whole milk and cream, with 10 to 12 percent fat. It cannot be whipped, and is used in cooking, baking, and coffee.

Best for whipping

Use heavy whipping cream. Make sure it's cold (if it's warm it can turn into butter). Cream is much easier to whip than egg whites—and also easier to overwhip. For that reason it's safest to use a handheld whisk, not anything electric. A handheld whisk will also create the lightest foam. If you are making it in advance and putting it back in the refrigerator, always underwhisk it because it will harden a little while resting.

Whipping: The fun method

If you want to make a really classic banana split and generally be childish with cream, you can buy a cream squirter. This looks a little like an old-fashion soda fountain, and is powered by tiny canisters of nitrous oxide. Use it to whip the cream up into foamy swirled peaks—and to squirt cream directly into your mouth, like when you were eight. We use them for our Leon Salted Caramel Banana Split (see page 281). Warning 1: This cream is unstable and will turn back to liquid within half an hour (unlike cream whipped with a whisk), so squirt it at the last minute. Warning 2: Nitrous oxide is commonly known as laughing gas (or, on the labor ward, as "gas and air") and can produce a euphoric effect if inhaled directly from the whipper. Do not try this unless you are giving birth and there is a nurse present.

6 PASTRY—BASIC

General tips

When making most pastries, the trick is to trap little pieces of butter within a dough, which melt when you cook it and create something flaky and delicious as the water from the butter evaporates and turns to steam, which rises, pushing up the layers. Unless otherwise stated, therefore, make sure that all your ingredients are cold and that you make it in a cold room (if the butter melts before you cook it, you will get something dense instead of light and flaky pastry).

Always rest a dough in the refrigerator for at least half an hour before rolling it out. (This lets the gluten relax, which will make the task much easier).

When rolling out dough for a tart pan, lift the pressure as you get to the edge of the dough to avoid making it too thin.

Your pastry will vary depending on the type of flour you use, the fats, the humidity, the temperature, etc. If you are eager to perfect the art, observe closely what happens each time you make a certain type of pastry and take notes. Over time you will learn when an extra splash of water or a sift of flour are required.

Basic pastries

The basic kinds of pastries that we use in this book are pressed-crust pastry, and two versions of flaky pastry. Pressed-crust pastry and the first version of flaky pastry crumble into small pieces, because the fat has been worked through the flour. The second version of flaky pastry has thin layers of fat and dough that will break into thin flakes. Recipes for these are with the main recipes as appropriate. (In addition to these you can find a hot-water crust recipe with the pork pie on page 284).

Henry thinks life is a bit too short to be making your own puff pastry—you can now buy some very good ready-to-bake versions from the supermarket.

Pressed-crust dough

Makes enough for
an 8–9-inch tart pan

1 cup plus 2 tablespoons **all-purpose flour**
2 tablespoons **superfine sugar**
7 tablespoons **unsalted butter**, melted
1 tablespoon **white vinegar**

1. Blend the ingredients briefly in a food processor and pat
    into a tart pan.

Flaky pastry dough I

Makes enough for
a 9-inch pie crust

1⅔ cups **all-purpose flour**
a pinch of **salt**
5 tablespoons **unsalted butter**, in ½-inch cubes
2½ tablespoons **cold water**

1. Sift the flour and salt and add the butter. Mix gently until
    the mixture resembles coarse sand.

2. Sprinkle the water over the mixture and mix until it forms a
    cohesive ball of dough.

3. Wrap the dough in plastic wrap and let rest in the
    refrigerator for at least 30 minutes before using.

Flaky pastry dough II

The same ingredients as above but keep the pieces of butter
larger and don't mix them in all the way.

⑦ MAKING CAKES

Slow & low
If in doubt when making a cake, bake it slow and low for greater moistness throughout. The name of this method came from a rap song that Claire is particularly fond of. "Slow and low that is the tempo" is the lyric, and it has become her baking mantra.

To test for doneness
There are three ways to test for doneness.

The toothpick method: Good for denser cakes. Insert a toothpick (or a long, thin knife) into the center of the cake, and when it pulls out clean, the cake is done.

The listening method: Henry's mother-in-law, Petra (see page 274), swears by this for fruitcakes. Open the oven door, take out the cake and listen to it. A fruitcake will "hiss" gently while it cooks. When it stops hissing, it is done.

The pressing method: Good for lighter cakes such as sponges. Press down gently on the top of the cake; when it springs back, instead of leaving a slight dent, it is done.

⑧ ICING & FROSTING

There are three main toppings that we use in this book: basic icing, royal icing, and buttercream.

Basic icing is simply a mixture of water (or more often fruit juice or puree) and confectioners' sugar, and forms a delicate, flat, slightly crispy coating when set.

Royal icing is similar to basic icing, but uses egg white to make it harden to a much more brittle texture (think Christmas cake).

Buttercream (think cupcakes) is a rich and creamy mixture of sugar, butter, and flavorings. Claire has also come up with vegan vanilla frosting—a version of buttercream using coconut oil, soy milk, and agave nectar in place of butter and sugar. It rocks.

You can find recipes for icings and frostings on the pages below:

⑨ STORING

Cakes, bread & cookies
These should all be wrapped in wax paper and kept in an airtight container at room temperature. Storing them in the refrigerator will make them turn stale more quickly (starches crystallize faster at colder temperatures). Bread freezes well. Try slicing it and storing it in airtight bags, then toasting it straight from the freezer.

Baking ingredients
Ingredients that live in the refrigerator are best kept in an airtight container to stop them from picking up smells from other foods. It's also best to keep flour, sugar and other pantry ingredients in airtight containers to keep the damp out.

⑩ DOUGH

Kneading
When kneading dough by hand, remember that you are trying to stretch the gluten. This requires energy. Henry likes to break a sweat

when making and baking bread. He says if you are not breaking a sweat, you are not working it hard enough. Big, long stretches with the ball of the hand are the thing. Claire is a fan of the slap and tickle method: stretching the dough up and out, then slapping it down on to a work surface rather than using the pushing method. The idea with this method is to incorporate air into the dough while kneading and to form the gluten so that you don't need to add as much flour to the bread. Both methods will produce equally beautiful bread.

⑪ FRUIT

Juicing
There are three ways to juice a fruit: using an electric juicer (for hard fruit, such as apples); using a squeezer or reamer (citrus fruit); and using a strainer (for soft berries, such as raspberries, which can easily be forced through a strainer with the back of a metal spoon).

Zesting
Make sure you don't zest any of the bitter pith. Also, zest over a bowl in order to catch the highly flavored oils that squirt out during the process.

Preparing mango

Use a large knife to slice the mango in half (Fig. 1), cutting either side of the large, flattish pit in the middle. With a smaller paring knife, score the flesh in lines and then crosswise (Fig. 2), so that you have a crisscross pattern. Invert the slice of mango so that the cubes of flesh are sticking out (Fig. 3), and cut them into a bowl. To avoid wasting any flesh, work around the pit—cut off any remaining flesh from the top and bottom and add to your stash.

Preparing pomegranates

Slice the top off the pomegranate (like taking the lid off a pumpkin at Halloween). Invert the pomegranate over a bowl and tap it with the back of a wooden spoon. The seeds will pop right out! Pomegranate juice is pretty squirty and deeply colored, so protect your clothes and any porous surfaces.

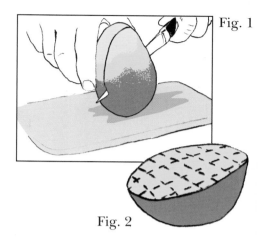

Fig. 1

Fig. 2

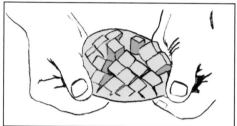

Fig. 3

Opening a coconut

Use a hammer and nail or an awl, and tap the tip of the sharp end into each of the three black "eyes" in the end of a coconut. Invert the coconut over a glass and let the water drain out. Drink the water. It is so good for you. Once it has drained, place the coconut on its side on a dish towel that has been folded a few times.

One end of the coconut is slightly more bulbous. Use a hammer to tap the perimeter of the coconut at its fattest point. A natural fracture should occur. The coconut will then quite easily open up.

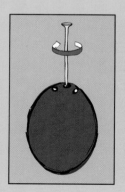

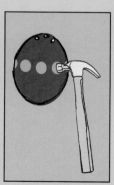

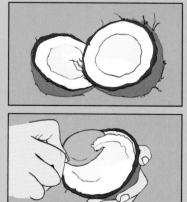

11 FIRST AID
WHAT TO DO WHEN IT GOES WRONG

Curdled butter & eggs

To help avoid curdling, always bring your ingredients to room temperature before you start. Your butter should be very, very soft. Whip the butter and sugar together with an electric handheld mixer. It is so much easier than doing it by hand, and you will get enough air into the mixture to be able to hold the eggs. The butter and sugar mixture is ready when it has doubled in volume and turned almost white.

Add the eggs one by one, completely incorporating each addition.

If you're making a cake that has a lot of eggs (such as a layer cake), add a teaspoon or two of flour to help stabilize the mixture, but not too much or the cake may become tough.

Sunken cakes

If a cake has baking soda in it and no acid (e.g. cream of tartar) to neutralize it, it can rise in the beginning and then fall down. (Note: if a recipe calls for baking powder, a mix of baking soda and cream of tartar can be substituted.)

Always check the expiration dates on your leavening powders. They don't last forever, and expired leavening powders are the source of many failed cakes.

Too much mixture in the cake pan can cause a cake to sink in the middle. When baking a sponge, always leave about a quarter of the pan unfilled to give the cake room to rise up. Fruitcakes won't rise as much, so you can fill the pan a bit more.

Sinking can also be a sign that your cake is underbaked. See Testing Doneness.

Testing doneness

Be sure to use the right method to test for doneness (see page 39), because not every method works for every cake.

Some cakes are meant to be moist, so the toothpick test isn't foolproof. The spring-back-to-the-touch test is not always sufficient if a cake is supposed to be soft. The "listening" method works best for fruitcakes, and the timer is never to be trusted.

Take notes on recipes—if you make a mistake the first time, you will know better next time around. It is important to learn to trust your instinct.

Try not to rush the cooling of a cake. As a cake cools, it continues to bake very slightly. Rushing it might mean it sinks instead.

Blind baking

Line your tart pan with the dough, then be sure to chill it for at least 20 minutes in the refrigerator or 10 minutes in the freezer. This helps to keep the dough from slumping down the sides.

Line the dough with buttered parchment paper or a silicone-lined parchment paper that won't stick to it. Fill it right to the top of the shell with pie weights, dried beans, or rice. Once the shell has baked enough to hold its shape, remove the weights and paper and continue to bake until just golden.

If you want to keep the pastry on the lighter side, cover it loosely with aluminum foil or parchment paper as it cooks. If you are using a convection oven this can be difficult, because the fan will blow the paper about.

Convection ovens

Often cookbooks will ask you to put the cake in the middle of the oven, because heat rises and the top can be hotter than the bottom. Modern convection ovens are very efficient at circulating heat evenly around the oven, so there's no need to worry about positioning. Even if you have a few racks filled, the heat will be pushed by the fan all around the baking cakes.

All the recipes in this book have been tested without a fan, with the cakes positioned on the middle shelf of the oven. If you are using a convection oven, lower the given temperature by 25°F.

Meringues

The trick to making successful meringues is to open the oven door a few times during the baking to let condensation out. The idea is to dry out the exterior of the meringues while keeping the inside moist.

(The recipe for Pavlova on page 140 also adds cornstarch and vinegar to help create that chewy centre.)

Baking powder & all-purpose flour *vs.* self-rising

If you only have all-purpose flour on hand and a recipe calls for self-rising, you can add 1½ teaspoons of baking powder and ½ teaspoon salt for every 1 cup of all-purpose flour.

Substitute for buttermilk

Buttermilk and yogurt make cakes soft and moist because of their acidity. If you don't have buttermilk, you can use half plain yogurt and half whole milk. Another alternative is to use 1 tablespoon of fresh lemon juice with 1 cup of milk—this will make the equivalent of 1 cup of buttermilk.

Substitute for brown sugar

If you have no brown sugar, add 1 tablespoon of molasses to 1 cup of granulated sugar to get the right flavor.

Rolling/patching pastry (when hot)

If you blind bake a pastry shell and find it has small holes or cracks when it comes out of the oven, you can patch it while still hot with scraps left over from rolling. When the patches of raw dough hit the hot pastry, they cook and form little seals.

Domed cakes/muffins

There are two main reasons why cakes sometimes dome up in the middle.
(a) The metal on the outside of the pan conducts the heat faster. The sides of the cake set while the center still continues to bake and rise.
(b) The structure of the cake is too strong, preventing the leavening gases from escaping until toward the end of baking, when they erupt through the center in little tunnels. The batter may have been mixed too much after the flour was added, and the air bubbles try to escape through the middle. When glutens form, the crumb becomes dry and tough.

ADVANCED TECHNIQUES

① STERILIZING JARS

To sterilize, put clean, washed, and dried jam jars or bottles into a cold oven with the lids off. Turn the oven on to 340°F and put the timer on for 20 minutes. When the bell goes, turn off the oven, leaving the jars inside. Pour in your jam, jelly, chutney, or syrup while the jars are still hot.

② CHOCOLATE—ADVANCED

Tempering

Although it looks all smooth, the chocolate we eat is given its shine and "snap" by the crystalline structure of cocoa butter. Unfortunately, the butter can crystallize in six ways and only one of them is the right kind. You will notice that if you take a bar of chocolate, melt it and then let it reset, it will be dull in color and soft, because the crystals have reformed the wrong way. This doesn't matter when you are using chocolate in cakes and so on. But if you want to make, say, an Easter egg with the proper shine and snap, you have to "temper" it to ensure the crystals set right. There are three ways to do this.

Thermometer method

Requires concentration, but foolproof.

1. Place 6oz chocolate in a bowl. Bring a pan of water to a boil and remove it from the heat. Place the bowl of chocolate over the steaming water. Melt the chocolate, stirring, until it registers 115°F with a candy or chocolate thermometer.

2. Let it sit for 10 minutes and stir again. While it is sitting, chop another 2oz of chocolate into finer pieces. Add this by spoonfuls to the melted chocolate, stirring until completely smooth each time.

3. You are trying to get the chocolate to 86°F. You may not need all the chocolate. (If you have lumps, use an immersion blender to smooth it out).

4. Bring your pan back to a boil and remove it from the heat.

5. Place your bowl of chocolate over it for a few seconds to bring it up to 90°F.

Tempering machine

By far the easiest method. Just chuck the chocolate into the machine. It does the rest. If you live in a big city, you may find that you can rent one.

The marble slab method

This is how artisanal chocolate makers do it. It is a lot of fun, really messy (see pictures on page 216), and quite hard. We would strongly recommend finding someone to teach you. You will need a marble or stone slab (at least 1 inch thick). It must be uniformly cool, so make sure that you do not have a dishwasher running underneath it, and do not place anything hot (such as a cup of coffee) on it.

Melt a large quantity of chocolate in the oven at 122°F maximum for dark chocolate, 104–113°F for white or milk chocolate (you will need an accurate oven to be sure of the temperature). Pour a quarter of the chocolate on to the slab. Swish it around using a dough scraper and a spatula. It is important to keep the chocolate around the worktop so that none of it starts to set, and it all cools evenly. Periodically touch the chocolate to your lip. When it feels slightly cooler than body temperature (it will be the texture of cake batter), pour it back into the bowl and mix it into the remaining chocolate. Work fast.

BAKING WITH ALTERNATIVES

Baking with alternatives to wheat flour, butter, and white sugar is easier than you might think. Think of these alternatives not as replacement ingredients but as new ones to experiment with. If you don't go in much for experimentation in the kitchen, don't worry; we have done most of the work for you already. All tried and tested, and this is one situation where curiosity definitely won't kill the cat.

If you want to be more experimental, try using these ingredients in your own recipes. You may need a bit of good old-fashioned trial and error before they work out, but to help you, here are some general rules that will let you predict how they may behave.

Flours

Rice flour is a great alternative to wheat if used in conjunction with a little xanthan gum, which is a good stand-in for gluten. Without it, cakes can crumble a bit too much. Rice flour has a slightly coarser texture to that of wheat flour. The finely ground rice has a crumbly texture that is similar to almond meal or ground almonds and different from the light texture of wheat flour. It lies somewhere between wheat and corn flour.

Although corn and oats are OK for some people, they are not suitable for everyone with a wheat and gluten intolerance. We have tried to include recipes for everyone. Some already-mixed gluten-free flours are an easy way to take your favourite recipe and make it suitable for you.

Sweeteners

Wherever caster sugar is called for, this is usually not just for sweetness but also for its structural qualities. For that reason, be cautious about using substitutes.

Agave nectar is a wonderful sweetener and much easier for our bodies to digest than sugar. It is also suitable for those who can't have sugar or honey. It takes longer to absorb into the bloodstream as well, so your blood sugar doesn't go haywire. We also love maple syrup, but it is very expensive.

Dairy & egg alternatives

Coconut oil is a very exciting discovery if you are staying away from dairy. It makes fantastic frosting (although you'll need to chill it a bit, because it stays liquid at a lower temperature than butter). It also works very well baked in some cakes.

If soy milk agrees with you, you'll find it great to bake with. Rice milk and coconut milk are very good, too, but a little different in texture. We use cashew nut butter in our vanilla frosting, along with soy (or rice) milk and coconut oil, and the creamy texture is a dream.

Egg alternatives are easier to find than you might expect. A little ground flaxseed meal or chia seed makes a great nutritional substitute. You can also use applesauce to get the right texture in cakes. Commercial egg replacers are usually just soy and potato starch, which are thickeners.

RICE FLOUR

EVERY DAY

**BREAKFAST • POWER SNACKS • TEA TIME
DESSERTS • COOKING WITH CHILDREN
BREAD & SAVORIES • SWEETS**

BREAKFAST

READY TO SERVE

GRANOLAS • MILKS • NUT BUTTERS • MUFFINS • PANCAKES • BREADS

The idea of baking for breakfast probably seems a little short of ludicrous.

Most of us are in such a hurry in the morning that it's all we can do to snatch a rusk from the baby's fist en route to the door. On the other hand, when you do have time to savor it, breakfast can be the most pleasurable meal of the day: your appetite is properly whetted by twelve hours without food, your taste buds are firing on all cylinders, and you don't even need to get dressed for the feast.

The recipes that follow cover both kinds of breakfast. You can make the superhealthy granola and breakfast spreads on the weekend and then wolf them during the week, and we have also included some more indulgent weekend treats.

MADE AT HOME

Our Favorite Granola

A wonderful, rich, versatile granola. Eat it with milk or put some on yogurt.

Makes: 3½ lbs (a good amount)
Preparation time: 10 minutes
Cooking time: 1 hour 40 minutes
❤ WF GF DF V

6½ cups **rolled oats**
1 cup **whole almonds** (skins on)
½ cup **ground flaxseeds**
⅓ cup **sesame seeds**
50ml **maple syrup**
½ cup **sunflower oil**
1 cup **honey**
¼ cup firmly packed **dark brown sugar**
¼ cup **water**
1½ teaspoons **pure vanilla extract**
½ teaspoon **ground cinnamon**
a grating of **fresh nutmeg**
a pinch of **sea salt**
1 cup sliced **dried apricots**
⅔ cup **golden raisins**
⅓ cup **dried sour cherries**

1. Heat the oven to 300°F. Line 2 baking sheets with parchment paper.

2. Put the oats, whole almonds, flaxseeds and sesame seeds in a large bowl and set aside.

3. In a saucepan, combine the maple syrup, sunflower oil, honey, dark brown sugar, and water. Place over medium heat and beat continuously to melt it all together without burning.

4. Remove the syrup mixture from the heat and stir in the vanilla, spices, and salt. Pour the syrup over the oat mixture and stir well to completely coat the oats, nuts, and seeds.

5. Spread out the mixture on the baking sheets and bake in the oven for 1 hour.

6. Remove from the oven, toss the mixture well with a metal spatula and return to the oven. Lower the temperature to 275°F, and bake for another 35–40 minutes, until the mixture is golden. Remove from the oven and let cool completely before stirring in the apricots, golden raisins and sour cherries.

 TIPS

❖ Granola will keep for weeks in an airtight container.

❖ You can replace the sugar and maple syrup with equal amounts of agave syrup for a low GI version.

Claire's Healthy Granola

You will not believe how good this tastes. It is light and clustery.

Makes: 3½ lbs (a good amount)
Preparation time: 10 minutes
Cooking time: 1 hour 40 minutes
❤ ✓ WF GF DF V

10 cups **buckwheat flakes**
1 cup **whole almonds** (skins on)
½ cup **ground flaxseeds**
⅓ cup **sesame seeds**
¼ cup **pumpkin seeds**
¼ cup **amaranth**
1 cup **agave syrup**
¼ cup **olive oil** (not extra virgin)
½ cup **coconut oil**
½ cup **water**
1½ teaspoons **vanilla extract**
½ teaspoon **ground cinnamon**
a grating of **fresh nutmeg**
a pinch of **sea salt**
⅔ cup **golden raisins**
¾ cup **dry, unsweetened shredded coconut**

I came up with this when I was on a cleanse, but I eat it all the time now. The buckwheat flakes have a wonderfully nutty flavour and the addition of coconut and olive oil makes it good for those avoiding certain fats. I love the crunch of amaranth too, another ancient grain.

CLAIRE

1. Heat the oven to 300°F. Line 2 baking sheets with parchment paper.

2. Put the buckwheat flakes, whole almonds, flaxseeds, sesame seeds, pumpkin seeds, and amaranth into a large bowl and set aside.

3. In a saucepan, combine the agave syrup, olive oil, coconut oil, and water. Place over medium heat and beat continuously to melt it all together without burning.

4. Remove the syrup mixture from the heat and stir in the vanilla, spices, and salt. Pour the syrup over the dry ingredients and stir well to completely coat all the nuts and seeds.

5. Spread out the mixture on the baking sheets and bake in the oven for approximately 1 hour.

6. Remove from the oven, toss the mixture well with a metal spatula, and return to the oven. Lower the temperature to 275°F, and bake for another 35–40 minutes, until the mixture is golden. Remove from the oven and let cool completely before stirring in the golden raisins and dry shredded coconut, then store in an airtight container.

TIPS

✤ Serve with fresh dates and low-fat plain yogurt for a naturally sweet treat.

Luxury Granola

This one has white chocolate in it.

Makes: about 4 lb
Preparation time: 10 minutes
Cooking time: 1 hour 40 minutes
♥ WF GF V

6½ cups **rolled oats**

1 cup **whole hazelnuts**

1 cup **pecans**

¼ cup **maple syrup**

½ cup **sunflower oil**

1 cup **honey**

½ cup firmly packed **brown sugar**

¼ cup **water**

1½ teaspoons **vanilla extract**

½ teaspoon **ground ginger**

a pinch of **sea salt**

3 tablespoons **light corn syrup**

1½ cups **jumbo dry, unsweetened shredded coconut**

7oz **white chocolate pieces**

1½ cups **dried blueberries**

1. Heat the oven to 300°F. Line 2 baking sheets with parchment paper.

2. Put the oats, hazelnuts and pecans into a large bowl and set aside.

3. In a saucepan, combine the maple syrup, sunflower oil, honey, brown sugar, and water. Place over medium heat and beat continuously to melt it all together without burning.

4. Remove the syrup mixture from the heat and stir in the vanilla, ground ginger, and salt. Pour this over the oat mixture and stir well to completely coat the oats, nuts and seeds.

5. Spread out the mixture on the baking sheets and cook in the oven for approximately 1 hour.

6. Remove from the oven, drizzle the mixture with the corn syrup and add the coconut. Toss well with a metal spatula and return the baking sheets to the oven. Lower the temperature to 275°F, and bake for another 30 minutes, until the mixture is golden. Remove from the oven and stir in the white chocolate. Let cool completely before folding in the blueberries and storing in an airtight container.

TIPS

❖ Really good sprinkled on top of storebought vanilla ice cream for an easy dessert.

Maggie's Milks

If milk doesn't agree with you, you're going to love these seed-based alternatives. Maggie (see page 232) taught Claire how to make them. Don't be put off because they sound whacky. They are delicate, sweet, and unbelievably good in their own right. Pour them on to your cereal or just glug them back from a glass.

Hazelnut Milk

Makes: about 2½ cups
Preparation time: 10 minutes +
soaking time overnight
Cooking time: none
♥ ✓ WF GF DF V

¾ cup **hazelnuts**, soaked overnight or for 8 hours in chlorine-free water, drained and rinsed
seeds from ¼ of a **vanilla bean**
2 tablespoons **raw honey** (preferably crystallized)
2½ cups **water**
a tiny pinch of **sea salt**

1. In a blender, blend the soaked hazelnuts, vanilla seeds and honey with 1 cup of the water until almost smooth.
2. Add the remaining water and blend to mix.
3. Strain through a nut milk bag, fine-mesh cheesecloth, or similar.
4. Chill and enjoy. Keeps for 6–8 days in the refrigerator.

Pumpkin Seed Milk

Makes: about 3¼ cups
Preparation time: 15 minutes +
soaking time overnight
Cooking time: none
♥ ✓ WF GF DF V

1½ cups **pumpkin seeds**, soaked overnight or for 6–8 hours in chlorine-free water, drained and rinsed
⅓ cup **cashews**, soaked overnight or for 6–8 hours in chlorine-free water, drained, and rinsed
2 **dates**, pitted
1 tablespoon **maple syrup**
6 strokes of grated **nutmeg** (optional)
a pinch of **sea salt**
3 cups **water**

1. In a blender, bend all the ingredients with 1¾ cups of the water until almost smooth.
2. Add the remaining water and blend together.
3. Strain through a nut milk bag, fine-mesh cheesecloth, or similar.
4. Chill and enjoy. Keeps for 6–8 days in the refrigerator.

TIPS

✤ To make this milk 100 percent raw, omit the cashew nuts, maple syrup, and ½ cup of water. Add 1 or 2 more dates.

Raw Nut & Seed Butters

One of the best things to spread on your bread first thing in the morning is a homemade nut butter. They are both indulgent and fantastically good for you.

Choose good-quality, very fresh raw walnuts, almonds, pumpkin seeds, hazelnuts, cashew nuts or sunflower seeds.

1. If you prefer, you can first soak or sprout the nuts or seeds. If you do this, make sure you dry them well before processing them.

2. Process the nuts or seeds in a food processor for several minutes to extract all the oil. As the nuts and seeds are being processed, you can drizzle in a little raw honey or water to help turn it into an emulsified butter.

3. Store in the refrigerator.

Salmon & Dill Muffins

A savoury breakfast muffin.

Makes: 6
Preparation time: 15 minutes
Cooking time: 20 minutes

2 cups **all-purpose flour**
2 teaspoons **baking powder**
1½ cups **grated cheese**
2oz chopped **smoked salmon**
⅓ cup chopped **fresh dill**
1 **free-range egg**
¾ cup **buttermilk**
⅓ cup **vegetable** or **sunflower oil**
½ cup **cream cheese**

Our friend Rebecca used to make these for us painstakingly every day at home and then drive them to the restaurants daily. Sadly (for us) she is now the proud mother of two and the muffins are no longer to be found in Leon. If you liked them, here they are.

HENRY

1. Heat the oven to 350°F, and line a 6-cup muffin pan with paper liners.

2. Mix together the flour and baking powder in a large bowl. Add the grated cheese, smoked salmon, and dill.

3. In a separate bowl, beat together the egg, buttermilk and oil.

4. Place half the wet ingredients into the dry ingredients and stir well. Then add the rest of the wet ingredients and mix until completely combined.

5. Spoon into the muffin liners until each is filled halfway, then place a heaping teaspoon of cream cheese in the middle of each muffin. Add more batter until they are full with mixture.

6. Cook for 10 minutes, then take the pan out and turn it around so the muffins cook evenly. Put the pan back into the oven and continue to cook for another 10 minutes, or until the muffins are just browning on top.

FRIENDS & FAMILY RECIPES

Rebecca on her 9th birthday
at home, 1982

Almond Date Oat Muffins

A nutty, semisweet breakfast muffin made with spelt flour, which is not only better for you than other varieties of wheat, but gives it its distinctive texture and flavor.

Makes: 12
Preparation time: 20 minutes
Cooking time: 25 minutes
♥ ✓ V

¾ cup **whole almonds**, skins on
1¾ sticks **unsalted butter**, melted
⅓ cup **light brown sugar**
2 cups **oat bran**
1 cup **rolled oats**, plus more to
   sprinkle the tops with
1¾ cups **fine spelt flour**
½ teaspoon **salt**
1½ teaspoons **baking soda**
2 **free-range eggs**
1½ cups **plain yogurt**
2 cups **pitted chopped dates**
zest from 1 **orange**

This muffin is inspired by one I learned to make at the wonderful Bovine Bakery, in Point Reyes, California. I started my career there, at the age of 15, under the tutelage of Deborah Ruff and Bridget Devlin. I learned so much from them, not only about baking but about running a small business. This muffin is my homage to them.

CLAIRE

1. Heat the oven to 340°F. Butter a muffin pan or line it with paper liners.

2. Spread out the almonds on a baking sheet and toast in the oven for 5–7 minutes, or until golden.

3. Melt the butter and sugar in a small saucepan and set aside to cool slightly.

4. In a large bowl, mix together the oat bran, rolled oats, spelt flour, salt and baking soda. Coarsely chop the toasted almonds and stir them into the dry ingredients.

5. In a new bowl, beat together the eggs and yogurt and stir in the dates and orange zest. Beat in the melted butter and sugar and pour all of this over the dry ingredients. Mix just until combined.

6. Spoon the batter into the muffin pan and bake in the oven for 20–25 minutes.

TIPS

✦ You could also make these muffins with dates that have been soaked in juice or alcohol.

COCKADOODLEDOO

RISE & SHINE

Saturday Pancakes

A little bit of Saturday morning indulgence.

Makes: about 12, enough for 4 people
Preparation time: 10 minutes
Cooking time: 5 minutes
V

For the pancakes
1¼ cups **all-purpose flour**
⅓ cup **sugar**
1½ teaspoons **baking powder**
¾ teaspoon **baking soda**
a pinch of **sea salt**
1 cup **plain yoghurt**
1 cup **milk**
3 **free-range eggs**
5 tablespoons **melted butter**

For the topping
maple syrup
berries

1. Combine the dry ingredients and set aside.

2. Combine the yogurt and milk and set aside.

3. Separate the eggs, add the yolks to the yogurt-milk mixture and stir to combine. Set the egg whites aside in a large, clean bowl.

4. In a steady stream, add the yogurt mixture to the flour and beat until smooth. Beat in the melted butter.

5. Beat the egg whites to stiff but not dry peaks and fold them into the batter.

6. Pour a pancake-size amount onto a hot griddle or skillet and cook for a couple of minutes on each side.

7. Stack them up and top with the syrup and the berries.

TIPS

✤ You can substitute buckwheat flour for the all-purpose flour if you want your pancakes to be gluten free.

French Toast

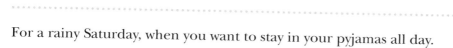

For a rainy Saturday, when you want to stay in your pyjamas all day.

Serves 4–6
Preparation time: 10 minutes
Cooking time: 15 minutes
V

2 tablespoons **unsalted butter**,
   plus extra to serve
5 **free-range eggs**
1¾ cups **whole milk**
1 tablespoon pure **vanilla extract**
⅓ cup **superfine sugar**
½ teaspoon **ground cinnamon**
8–12 slices of good **stale bread**
confectioners' sugar, for dusting the top
maple syrup, to serve

This way of using up stale bread is almost as old as civilization itself (it features in a cookbook from fourth-century Rome). Every nation has a different name for it. The British call it eggy bread; the French *pain perdu*, the Czechs *chleba v kozíšku* ("bread in the little coat"). In Sri Lanka it's called Bombay toast, and in Germany *armer Ritter*, meaning "poor knights"— presumably because it was eaten by impoverished noblemen who couldn't afford fresh bread. This dish is a universal classic for a reason—it has been tried and tested and found to be absolutely delicious.

HENRY

1. Heat a large heavy skillet and drop in a little of the butter.

2. In a large shallow bowl, beat together the eggs, milk, vanilla, sugar, and cinnamon.

3. Place a couple of slices of bread in the eggy mixture and dunk it down, piercing the slices with tiny holes. Once the bread seems saturated, flip the slices over.

4. The skillet should now be ready and the butter sizzling.

5. Carefully lift the slices of bread from the eggy mixture and place in the skillet.

6. Brown the bread well on both sides, meanwhile repeating the dunking process with the remaining slices of bread.

7. Place on a plate, set in a warm place, and butter the slices.

8. Dust the finished slices of buttered French toast with confectioners' sugar and serve with maple syrup.

TIPS

❖ You can use all types of white crusty bread, as well as sourdough, if you prefer.

❖ Be sure to soak the bread with a lot of the eggy mixture. Don't be shy with the butter in the skillet. You want a moist, custardlike middle and a crisp exterior.

❖ Serve with fresh berries in the summer.

❖ Try slices of ripe bananas with a pinch of cinnamon.

❖ Add orange or lemon zest to the eggy mixture for a nice, bright flavour.

Hannah's* Banana Bread

A version of the classic bread made with spelt flour and a banana that sinks into the bread during cooking. This is the best banana bread we have tasted.

Serves: 8–10
Preparation time: 25 minutes
Cooking time: 50 minutes
 ♥ ✓ V

½ cup **pecans**
⅔ cup **vegetable oil**
1 cup firmly packed **dark brown sugar**
1 teaspoon **vanilla extract**
2 **free-range eggs**
4 ripe **bananas**, peeled
⅓ cup **plain yoghurt**
1 teaspoon **baking soda**
1 teaspoon **baking powder**
½ teaspoon **ground cinnamon**
¼ teaspoon **salt**
2 cups **whole-grain spelt flour**
1 **banana**, peeled, and 3 tablespoons **superfine sugar**, for the top

I invented this for Leon, when they were looking for a spelt version of this classic quick bread. The texture of the spelt flour and the nutty taste it imparts work so well with banana.

CLAIRE

*Some time ago people started leaving wishes on pieces of paper in a drawer in the Ludgate Circus branch of Leon. We celebrated this by granting the wishes of people who came to one of our parties. Hannah's wish was to have a cake named after her. Hence the name.

HENRY

1. Heat the oven to 340°F. Butter a 9 inch loaf pan and line it with parchment paper. Line a baking sheet with parchment paper as well.

2. Spread out the pecans over the lined baking sheet and toast them in the oven for about 5–7 minutes, or until lightly golden and fragrant. Set aside to cool.

3. In a large bowl, beat together the oil, dark brown sugar, vanilla and eggs.

4. In a separate bowl, coarsely mash up the bananas. Add the yogurt and mix well. Sift the baking soda, baking powder, and cinnamon over the yogurt mixture, add the salt, and stir well to combine.

5. Now, add the banana mixture to the egg mixture and stir to combine. Chop the pecans into small pieces and add them with the flour, stirring just until incorporated. Spoon the batter into the prepared loaf pan.

6. Carefully slice the remaining banana in half lengthwise. Place one half, cut side up, on top of the bread and sprinkle with the superfine sugar. (Eat the other half.)

7. Bake in the oven for 45–50 minutes, or until the bread is springy to the touch and a toothpick inserted comes out clean. Cool in the pan for at least 10 minutes before turning it out onto a wire rack to cool.

TIPS

❖ Never overmix the batter for quick breads like this, because they can easily turn tough and rubbery—I have a tendency to undermix them. The sugar on top makes a nice crunchy crust, but if you want to cut the sugar, just leave it out.

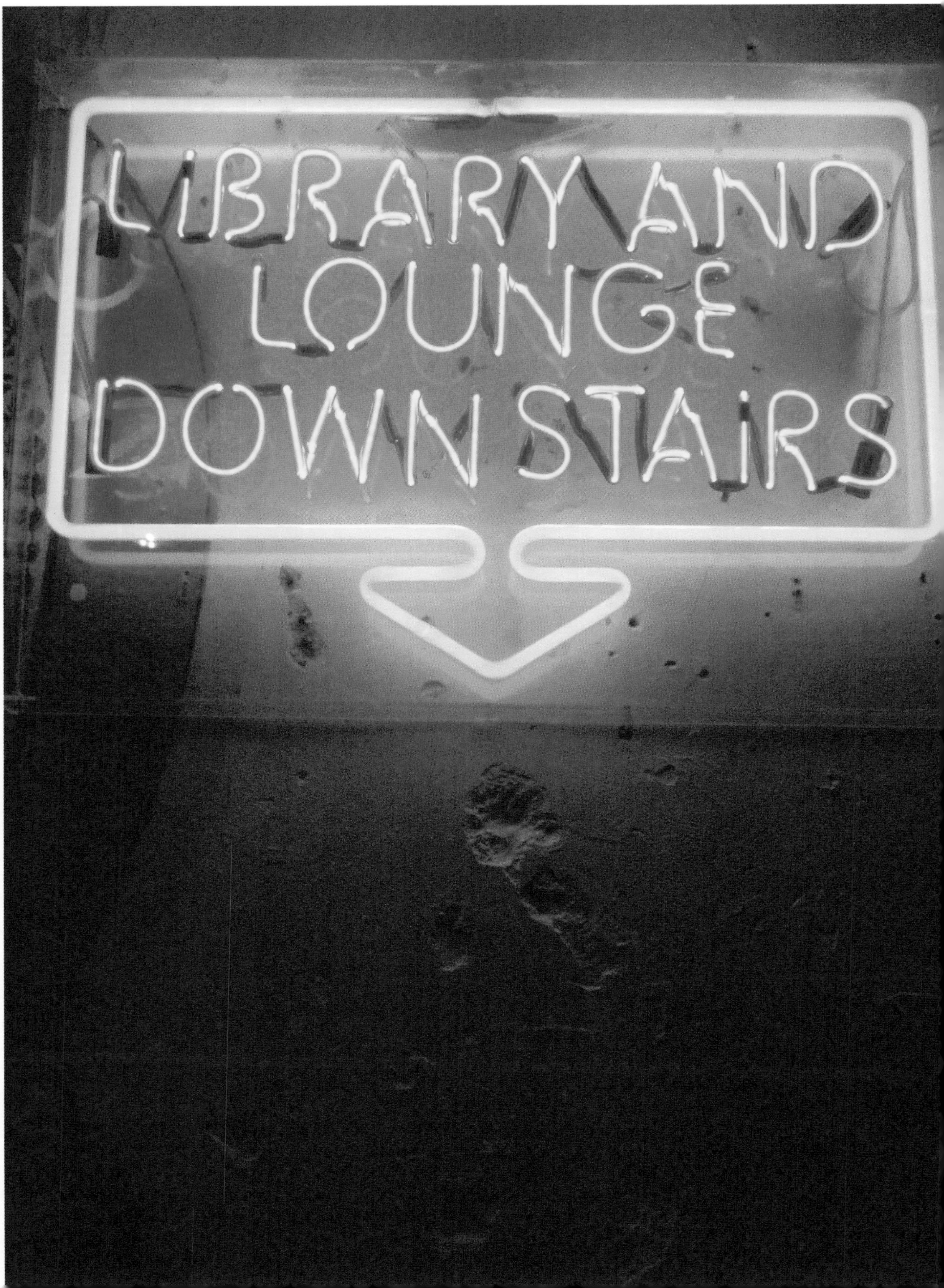
LIBRARY AND
LOUNGE
DOWN STAIRS

When we were putting together the first menus for Leon, we were aware that a lot of fast food, although superficially satisfying, actually makes you even hungrier. Foods that are full of refined carbohydrates make your blood sugar soar and then crash, leaving you craving more of the same.

Processed snacks tend to be particularly villainous in this respect. You want something wholesome to tide you over between lunch and dinner—something that will release energy slowly, instead of making you fall asleep at your desk— but you end up buying a slab of wheat and white rice glued together with corn sugar and marketed as a healthy "cereal bar".

Not so with these homemade power snacks. Low GI and stuffed full of good things, they will keep well in an airtight container, so you can make batches in advance to keep your lunch bag interesting for a good couple of weeks.

POWER SNACKS

BARS * COOKIES
BALLS * BROWNIES

FREE FROM GUILT

Claire's Chocolate Hazelnut Power Pills

These pocketable snacks taste sensational and give you a powerful burst of energy.
Make a huge batch and give some to your friends.

Makes: 12 balls or 24 power "pills"
Preparation time: 15 minutes
Cooking time: none
♥ ✓ WF GF DF V

½ cup **raw hazelnut butter**
¾ cup **Brazil nuts**, finely chopped
⅓ cup **dried cherries**, preferably
without oil or sweetener added,
finely chopped
2 tablespoons **shelled hemp seeds**
1 tablespoon **chia seeds**, ground
in a mortar
3 teaspoons **cacao nibs**, chopped
2 teaspoons **raw cacao powder**
3 teaspoons **raw honey**
1 teaspoon **maca root powder**
1 teaspoon **coconut oil**
½ teaspoon **blue green algae,
spirulina**, or **other source of
chlorophyll**
seeds from ¼ of a **vanilla bean**
extra **cacao powder**, **hemp seeds**, **chia seeds**
or **coconut shreds**, for coating

The Americas are a very
fertile land, and the ancient
civilizations that lived there
knew of the many health
properties of the roots, fruits,
seeds, and herbs that grew
there. Some of these plants—
like chia seeds and maca
root—are being rediscovered,
and many of them are
becoming widely available.
There is good information
on the Internet if you want to
learn more about their health
benefits. Be brave and
experiment with them.
The flavors and textures
are fascinating.

CLAIRE

1. Mix all the ingredients together in a bowl (easiest done using your hands).

2. Shape the paste into balls or pills and gently roll them
in the extra cacao powder, hemp seeds, chia seeds,
coconut shreds, or a combination of any of these.

3. Chill for 15 minutes. Keep refrigerated.

Lise's Cherry Almond Cookies with Chocolate Chips

The recipe below is based on Lise's oat and raisin cookie, which we serve in the restaurant, but with a sweet summer twist to it. If you want to make a version of the original, just replace the choc chips, cherries, and almonds with raisins (see picture).

Makes: 15–20 cookies
Preparation time: 20 minutes
Cooking time: 10–12 minutes

V

1¾ sticks **salted butter**, softened
1 cup firmly packed **brown sugar**
2 small **free-range eggs**
1 cup **all-purpose flour**
½ teaspoon **baking soda**
2 cups **rolled oats**
1 cup **dried sour cherries**
½ cup **slivered almonds**
½ cup **chocolate chips**

Lise learned to love baking in her mother's kitchen. Her mother had a fruit and vegetable garden outside her kitchen in the Danish countryside, next to the wild pine forests that sloped gently down to the sea. Everything was organic in her mother's kitchen, and still is now, in Lise's Honeyrose Bakery.

1. Heat the oven to 350°F. Oil several large baking sheets or line them with parchment paper.

2. Cream together the butter and the sugar, then add the eggs, one at a time, and beat until light and fluffy.

3. In another bowl, combine the flour, baking soda, oats, cherries, slivered almonds, and chocolate chips. Add to the butter mixture, being careful not to overmix the dough.

4. Scoop the dough into balls about 2 inches in diameter, using an ice cream scoop. You can also use 2 tablespoons. Place the dough balls on the prepared baking sheets 10 inches apart. Each cookie will spread to about 4 inches. If your dough is cold, the cookies will not spread as well, in which case you will need to press them with the palm of your hand before baking.

5. Bake in the oven for 10–12 minutes, or until golden (you may need to bake them in batches). The cookies will be very soft when you take them out, but will become firmer as they cool down. Let them cool on the baking sheets for a few minutes before transferring them to a wire rack to cool completely. Store in an airtight container.

FRIENDS & FAMILY RECIPES

Lise Madsen, Denmark, 1977

Nana Goy's Cranberry Oat Bars

These are moist and deliciously oaty like a good oat bar should be. We love them with dried cranberries but you could use any dried fruits (see tips below).

Makes: 16
Preparation time: 10 minutes
Cook time: 30–35 minutes
V

1½ cups **dried cranberries**

¼ cup **light corn syrup**

1½ sticks **butter**

½ cup **superfine sugar**

2¾ cups **rolled oats**

1. Heat the oven to 340°F, and butter an 8 inch square baking pan.

2. Put the cranberries into a bowl and cover with boiling water for a few minutes to rehydrate them. Drain away the water and coarsely chop any that are particularly large.

3. Melt together the syrup, butter, and sugar in a large saucepan over a low heat until the sugar has dissolved, then stir in the oats. Add all but a small handful of the cranberries and stir thoroughly.

4. Transfer the oat mixture into the pan and smooth it down with a spatula. Sprinkle the remaining cranberries on top. Bake in the oven for 30–35 minutes, until golden. Mark into squares while still warm, and remove from the pan once cool.

TIPS

✤   Add a handful of nuts and seeds to the mixture if you want to add another dimensions to your oat bars.

✤   For a fruity hit, try making them with dates instead of cranberries. If you choose to do this alternative, chop the dates coarsely before adding to the oat mixture.

Nana Goy with grandchildren,
West Clandon, 1980

Better Brownie

We have been selling these brownies at Leon since we opened our first restaurant in London's Carnaby Street in 2004. Made in Dorset by one of our favorite bakers, Emma Goss-Custard, it is sugar and wheat free, but incredibly luxurious. Emma's stroke of genius was to add the little chunks of chocolate, providing the perfect contrast to the rich, gooey interior.

Makes: 12 large brownies
Preparation time: 25 minutes
Cooking time: 25 minutes
WF GF

1½ sticks **unsalted butter**, plus extra for greasing
7oz **semisweet chocolate** (54% cocoa solids)
1 **orange**
2 teaspoons **espresso** or **strong coffee**
½ cup whole **almonds (skins on)**
4 free-range **eggs**
1 cup **almond meal (ground almonds)**
7oz **semisweet chocolate** (54% cocoa solids), in chunks
7oz **bittersweet chocolate** (70% cocoa solids), in chunks
¾ cup **fructose**
a pinch of **sea salt**
3–4 drops of **vanilla extract**

1. Heat the oven to 350°F. Generously butter a 12 x 8 x 2 inch baking pan, or one of similar dimensions.

2. Melt the butter in a small saucepan, and let it cool slightly.

3. In a separate bowl, melt the 7oz of chocolate over a saucepan of hot water, stirring well to make sure that it is properly melted, and being careful not to burn it. Finely grate the orange zest directly into the melted chocolate to catch the oils that are released during the zesting process.

4. Add the coffee to the melted butter.

5. Spread out the almonds on a baking sheet and toast in the oven for 10 minutes, then coarsely chop.

6. Crack the eggs into a large mixing bowl. Add the almond meal, the chopped almonds, all the chocolate chunks and finally the fructose. Stir in the salt and vanilla, followed by the butter mixture, and the melted chocolate.

7. Mix well until creamy and thickened, but do not overmix, because too much air will cause the brownie to crumble when baked.

8. Spoon the mixture into the prepared baking pan and place in the oven for approximately 20–25 minutes. Be careful not to overbake the brownies. They are ready when the edges are slightly crusty but the middle is still soft.

9. Remove from the oven and let cool in the pan.

❖ Fructose turns a much darker color when baked than sugar. The brownie develops a glossy sheen and will not look cooked, when, in fact, it is. Resist the temptation to cook it for too long.

❖ You can replace the fructose with 1 cup of sugar.

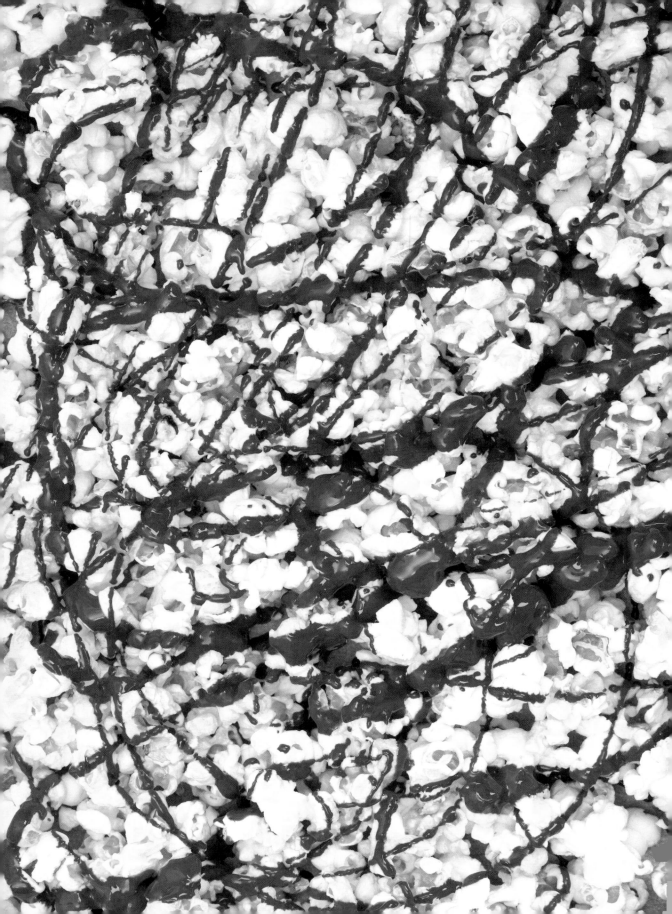

Sweet Popcorn with Chocolate Drizzle

A rainy Sunday afternoon snack that's almost as much fun to make as it is to eat. Make it alongside a salty popcorn and settle down on the coach with a good movie.

Serves: 4
Preparation time: 20 minutes
Cooking time: 10 minutes
♥ ✓ WF GF

2 tablespoons **vegetable oil**
¾ cup **popping corn**
4oz **semisweet chocolate**, broken into pieces
5 tablespoons **salted butter**
¼ cup **light corn syrup**

1. In a large saucepan with a tight-fitting lid, warm the oil over medium heat. Pour the popping corn into the saucepan and cover it with the lid. The corn will begin to pop quickly. When the popping slows down, by which time most of the kernels should have popped, remove the pan from the heat and open the lid to release the steam. Set aside.

2. Melt the chocolate in a small heatproof bowl over a saucepan of barely simmering water, making sure the water does not touch the surface of the bowl. Stir occasionally. Meanwhile line a baking sheet with parchment paper.

3. Melt together the butter and light corn syrup in another saucepan, stirring continuously.

4. Fold the popped corn into the syrup and stir well to coat. Spread the popcorn out to cool on the baking sheet.

5. When the chocolate has melted, drizzle it over the sweet popcorn.

TIPS

❖ Don't worry about shaking the pan around on the stove. Use a good heavy pot with a tight-fitting lid and you will get perfectly popped corn every time.

❖ Omit the light corn syrup if you want something less sweet.

Bar of Good Things

This recipe makes a healthy bar, and will keep you going on a long hike or make a great recharger after exercising.

Makes: 8 bars
Preparation time: 20 minutes
+ soaking time for seeds
Cooking time: 2 hours
♥ ✓ WF GF DF V

1 cup **sesame seeds**, preferably soaked and dried
1 cup **cashew nuts**, finely chopped
a pinch of **sea salt**
2 tablespoons **brown rice syrup**
2 tablespoons **tahini**
2 tablespoons **yacon syrup**
2 teaspoons **lemon zest**
1½ cups **salted pistachios**, shelled and coarsely chopped
⅔ cup chopped **dried apricots**,

For the fig paste
¼ cup **water**
1 teaspoon **vanilla extract**
 cup **dried figs**
1¼ teaspoons **ground ginger**
¼ teaspoon **ground cumin**

For the coating
½ cup **sesame seeds**, lightly toasted

1. Heat the oven to 225°F. Line a 12 x 8 inch baking pan with parchment paper.

2. Heat the water with the vanilla in a small saucepan and pour over the dried figs. Let rest for 15 minutes, then blend with the ginger and cumin to form a paste.

3. Meanwhile, mix the sesame seeds, cashew nuts and salt in a medium bowl.

4. Mix the brown rice syrup, tahini, yacon and lemon zest in a small bowl and stir in the fig paste.

5. Add the wet ingredients to the dry ingredients and mix well (this is easiest done with your hands, because the mixture should be stiff). Then fold in the pistachios and apricots.

6. Sprinkle half the sesame seeds for the coating into the prepared roasting pan and then press the mixture evenly on top so it is about ½ inch in thickness. Sprinkle over the remaining seeds.

7. Bake in the oven for 1 hour, then flip it over, put it back in the pan and bake for 1 more hour. Let cool in the pan. Cut into bars and keep in an airtight container.

TIPS

❖ The yacon syrup can be replaced by more brown rice syrup or agave nectar.

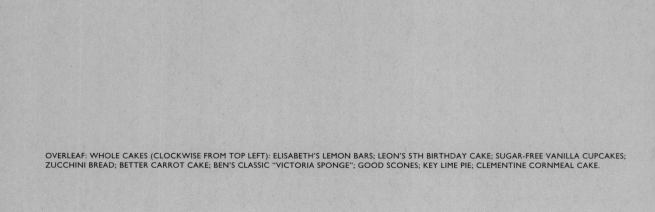

OVERLEAF: WHOLE CAKES (CLOCKWISE FROM TOP LEFT): ELISABETH'S LEMON BARS; LEON'S 5TH BIRTHDAY CAKE; SUGAR-FREE VANILLA CUPCAKES; ZUCCHINI BREAD; BETTER CARROT CAKE; BEN'S CLASSIC "VICTORIA SPONGE"; GOOD SCONES; KEY LIME PIE; CLEMENTINE CORNMEAL CAKE.

TEA TIME

Cakes, Tarts
& Breads

DELICATELY SCENTED

Ben's Classic "Victoria Sponge"

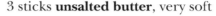

Classic recipes are classic because they have stood the test of time. "Victoria Sponge" is the traditional British name for this, the mother of all layer cakes.

Serves: 8
Preparation time: 25 minutes
Cooking time: 40 minutes

3 sticks **unsalted butter**, very soft

1¾ cups **superfine sugar**, plus more to finish

1 teaspoon **vanilla extract**

6 **free-range eggs**

2¾ cups **all-purpose flour**, with 4 teaspoons **baking powder**

½ cup homemade or store-bought **raspberry jam**

2 pints of **fresh raspberries** (if in season)

1½ cups **heavy cream**

1. Heat the oven to 325°F. Butter two 10 inch round cake tins and line them with baking parchment.

2. In a large mixing bowl, beat together the soft butter and the sugar until very pale and fluffy. Add the vanilla extract and the eggs, one at a time, alternating with 1 tablespoon of flour and beating well after each addition. Once all the eggs have been added, add the remaining flour and mix well.

3. Divide the mixture between the two pans and bake in the oven for about 40 minutes, or until a toothpick inserted in the center comes out clean.

4. Cool the cakes for at least 10 minutes in the pans before turning out onto a wire rack to cool completely.

5. Just before serving, place one cake on a serving plate and slather it with the raspberry jam. Whip the cream to very soft peaks—just stiff enough to start to hold a shape—and layer that over the jam, reserving a good dollop for the top of the cake. Scatter the raspberries over the cream (saving two or three for decoration) and finish with the second cake layer. Sprinkle with superfine sugar and put the last dollop of cream on top of the cake. Finish with the raspberries.

TIPS

✤ This cake is best eaten right away, but it can be kept in the refrigerator in an airtight container for up to 3 days.

✤ You can experiment with all kinds of different fruit fillings. Also try using Greek yogurt or crème fraîche instead of heavy cream.

 Our friend the actor Ben Miller was invited onto one of Gordon Ramsay's shows to compete against him in a bakeoff. To prepare himself, Ben had a day of intensive training with Claire, perfecting this cake. The key, Claire told him, was to bake it "slow and low" for a soft, yielding texture. The result? Ben beat Ramsay by a unanimous vote. Done.

WHEN WE ASKED BEN FOR A PICTUR
OF HIMSELF AS A BOY, HE SENT US T

Clementine Cornmeal Cake

This moist flourless cake is perfect for an afternoon treat, but also makes a beautiful dessert when drizzled with a little cream or topped with a blob of yogurt.

Serves: 12
Preparation time: 25 minutes
Cooking time: 50 minutes
WF GF

For the cake
2¼ sticks **unsalted butter**, very soft
1¼ cups **superfine sugar**
2 **free-range eggs**
1½ cups **cornmeal**
1 cup **almond meal**
1 teaspoon **baking powder**
zest and juice of 3 **clementines**
2 tablespoons **lemon juice**

For the syrup
¼ cup **honey**
juice of 1 **clementine** and 1 **lemon**

1. Heat the oven to 340°F. Butter a 10 inch round cake pan and line it with baking parchment.

2. In a large mixing bowl, beat the soft butter and sugar until very pale and fluffy. Add the eggs, one at a time, beating well after each addition.

3. In a separate bowl, beat together by hand the cornmeal, almond meal and baking powder. Add to the butter mixture and beat well. Fold in the clementine zest and juice and lemon juice before scraping the batter into your prepared pan.

4. Bake in the oven for 50 minutes, or until a toothpick inserted comes out clean.

5. To make the syrup, heat the honey with the clementine and lemon juice in a small saucepan over a low heat until runny, then pour over the cake while its still hot. Let cool in the pan.

TIPS

❖ Wonderful served with Greek yogurt or heavy cream.

❖ You can experiment with other kinds of citrus in this recipe as well. It works very well with lemon.

❖ You can also use agave nectar instead of honey for the syrup (this would go nicely with lime juice in place of the clemetines).

Petra's Fruitcake

Serves: 12–15

Preparation time: 40 minutes + soaking time

Cooking time: 3½–4 hours

V

1½ cups **golden raisins**

¼ cup **brandy**

1 cup good-quality **candied cherries**, quartered

1 cup good-quality **mixed peel**

¾ cup chopped **crystallized pineapple** or **papaya**

¾ cup finely chopped **crystallized ginger**

⅓ cup chopped **candied angelica**

1 cup **walnuts**

zest and juice of 1 **lemon**

2 sticks **unsalted butter**, softened

1 cup plus 2 tablespoons **superfine sugar**

4 **free-range eggs**, at room temperature

1⅓ cups **all-purpose flour**

½ teaspoon **salt**

1. Soak the raisins in the brandy for several hours or overnight. Chop the fruits and the walnuts, and mix with the raisins in a bowl.

2. Prepare a deep 9–10 inch cake pan—one with a loose bottom is best. Butter it and line it with 2 layers of parchment paper. To give the cake extra protection, tie a band of paper around the outside of the pan so that it sticks up an inch or so above the rim.

3. Just before you are ready to start making the cake, add the lemon zest and juice to the fruit.

4. Heat the oven to 325°F.

5. In a large bowl, cream the butter and sugar until pale and fluffy. In a separate bowl, beat the eggs really well with an electric handheld mixer until foamy, thick, and increased in volume—this may take up to 10 minutes, but it is worth it to get the right texture. Add the beaten eggs to the butter mixture a little at a time, beating well after each addition. (If the mixture shows any sign of curdling, beat in a tablespoon of the flour.) Stir in the remaining flour and then the salt.

6. Now you can stir in the prepared fruit and walnuts, a little at a time.

7. Transfer the batter to the prepared pan and smooth it over with the back of a spoon or a small metal spatula. Put the cake into the oven. After 1½ hours reduce the temperature to 275°F and bake for another 2 hours. After the cake has been in the oven for at least 2 hours, you can check to see if the top is browning too much. If it is, cover it with a double thickness of wax paper.

Petra & Hattie in Sussex, 1978

8. The cake is done when it is evenly risen, and brown, and has shrunk from the sides of the pan.

9. Let it cool in the pan, away from drafts, for at least an hour before taking it out. Let it cool completely before storing it in a large container.

TIPS

✤ Petra describes the slight hissing noise the cake makes while it is cooking (if you put your ear close to the pan) as "singing". You will know when the cake is done when the "singing" has stopped.

✤ This cake will work equally well as a christening or a wedding cake.

✤ Petra is a great cake baker, but not as great at frosting, so she disguises this deficit with increasingly extravagant decoration.

✤ The higher the quality of the crystallized fruit the better. Petra buys the whole crystallized ones from Harrods in London and chops them up herself (which might be going a bit far).

✤ Petra varies the recipe a little each year, to avoid getting bored. One of the nicest variations was the addition of 3 or 4 of the sugared apricots from Australia (not the ordinary dried ones). She cut down a little on the sugar and on the other fruit to compensate.

✤ Golden raisins are essential, beacause they are so pretty.

Petra is my wife Mima's mom (and one of our baking heroes—see page 274). This is the cake that my wife and her sister had at their christenings, at their weddings, and at the christenings of their own children. Word of its magnificence has spread, and with insane generosity Petra now seems to be in permanent production for friends and extended family.

HENRY

Tommi's More-Fruit-than-Cake Cake

Red wine and figs have a special affinity for one another and the spices in this recipe. The fig seeds create a wonderful popping sensation as they burst in your mouth.

Serves: 8
Preparation time: 25 minutes
Cooking time: 45 minutes
✓ V

1⅔ cups **red wine**
1¾ cups chopped **dried figs**
1½ teaspoons **ground cinnamon**
¼ teaspoon **ground cloves**
1 stick **unsalted butter**, cold
1 cup **honey**, plus extra for the top
1 **free-range egg**, briefly whisked
1¾ cups **spelt flour**
1½ teaspoons **baking powder**
1 teaspoon **baking soda**

One of the great things about Claire is that her world is overflowing with cake. This cake got its name when she was around at dinner with our friend and fellow cook Tommi Miers. There wasn't any dessert, but Claire happened to have this experiment in her car outside. Tommi hasn't stopped talking about it since— "Best cake I have ever had. Just sitting there. In her car!"

HENRY

1. Heat the oven to 325°F. Line an 8 inch square cake pan with parchment paper.

2. Put the red wine, figs, and spices into a medium saucepan and bring to a boil.

3. When the fruit has plumped up a little (about 5 minutes), remove the saucepan from the heat and let cool for 10 minutes. Stir in the butter and honey and let rest for another 10 minutes. Stir in the egg.

4. Sift the flour, baking power, and baking soda into a large mixing bowl. Pour the fig mixture over the flour mixture and stir until just mixed. Pour into the prepared pan.

5. Bake for about 45 minutes, or until a toothpick inserted into the center comes out clean. Let cool in the pan.

TIPS

❖ Serve with Greek yogurt or crème fraîche.

❖ A great way to use up leftover red wine.

❖ Can be served as a dessert or an afternoon snack. A chunk in the lunchbag also makes a great mid-morning snack.

FRIENDS & FAMILY RECIPES

Tommi in her modelling days, 1991

Elisabeth's Lemon Bars

Sweet and gooey, with a sharp finish. An indulgent treat.

Makes: 8–10
Preparation time: 30 minutes
Cooking time: 1 hour

2¼ cups **all-purpose flour**, plus an extra ¼ cup
⅔ cup **confectioners' sugar**
1 teaspoon **salt**
2 sticks **unsalted butter**
4 **free-range eggs**
1¾ cups **sugar**
½ cup **fresh lemon juice**
½ teaspoon grated **lemon zest**
1 teaspoon **baking powder**
confectioners' sugar to finish

1. Heat the oven to 340°F.

2. First make the shortbread crust. Combine the 2¼ cups flour, confectioners' sugar, salt, and cold butter in a food processor and mix until crumbly. If you don't have a food processor, cut the butter up with two knives (I always find this tricky), the back of a fork, or an old-fashion pastry cutter (I prefer the latter).

3. Be careful not to let the butter get too warm in either the appliance or your hands, because it changes the texture. Mix until the dough just forms a ball.

4. Press the dough into a 12 x 8 inch baking pan.

5. Bake in the oven for 20–25 minutes, or until golden and set, then let cool slightly while you make the topping.

6. Beat the eggs. Add the sugar, lemon juice, and lemon zest. In a separate bowl, sift together the remaining ¼ cup flour and the baking powder. Add to the egg mixture and stir to combine. Spread onto the cooled shortbread crust and return to the oven for 25–30 minutes, or until just set.

7. Cool completely in the pan. Sprinkle with confectioners' sugar and cut into squares or diamonds. These will keep well in an airtight container for up to 3 days.

 TIPS

❖ Sprinkle with lavender flowers if you have them growing in your yard.

My mom makes these for us with California Meyer lemons. I like to make them with Amalfi lemons because they have a similar sweetness, though the flavor is very different. They are my favorite treat. Judging by the speed at which they disappeared on the photo shoot for this book, I am not alone.

CLAIRE

Sugar-Free Vanilla Cupcakes

A cupcake free of everything except indulgence. No one will ever believe they are so good for you.

Makes: 12
Preparation time: 15 minutes
Cooking time: 25 minutes
♥ ✓ WF GF DF V

2¼ cups **gluten-free flour**
3¼ teaspoons **gluten-free baking powder**
100g **potato flour** (or **cornstarch**)
1 cup **coconut flour** (fine dry coconut)
1 tablespoon **flaxseed meal** (optional)
1½ teaspoons **sea salt**
⅔ cup **coconut oil**, melted
1 cup **agave nectar**
2 tablespoons **vanilla extract**
⅔ cup **rice milk**
½ teaspoon **baking soda**
½ cup **boiling water**

There is a bit of a craze for healthy cupcakes and muffins at the moment, but the recipes in the books we have seen in the past either don't work or have too many ingredients. This one works. Magnificently. And is a tribute to the many hours Claire spent perfecting it.

HENRY

1. Heat the oven to 340°F, and line a 12-cup muffin pan with paper liners.

2. Sift the gluten-free flour, baking powder, potato flour, coconut flour, flaxseed meal (if using) and sea salt into a large bowl, or use a whisk to mix them together.

3. In another bowl, combine the melted coconut oil, agave nectar, vanilla extract and rice milk. In a small bowl, mix together the baking soda and boiling water and then stir this into the other liquid ingredients.

4. Pour a third of the liquid ingredients into the dry and beat together to make a batter, gradually adding the remaining liquid until all of it is incorporated.

5. Spoon the batter into the paper liners and bake in the oven for 20–25 minutes, or until a toothpick inserted in the center of a cupcake comes out clean. These cakes are best eaten on the day they are made.

TIPS

✤ The flaxseed meal can be left out if you can't find it at your local health food store, but it adds nutrition and a nutty quality that we like, and also adds texture.

✤ If you don't like the flavor of coconut (you're crazy), you can replace the coconut flour with almond meal.

✤ The coconut oil can be replaced with a good-quality tasteless oil, such as sunflower, but only if you *really* must. Coconut oil is full of nutrition.

Vegan Vanilla Frosting

We think this frosting might be even better than the traditional buttercream version. It is the result of weeks spent by Claire testing different dairy- and allergen-free combinations. It is rich, but the coconut oil gives it a sublime melting consitency.

Makes: enough to frost 12 cupcakes
Preparation time: 15 minutes, plus cooling time in the refrigerator
Cooking time: none
♥ ✓ WF GF DF V

1½ cups **unsweetened soy milk**
1 cup **very finely ground almond**
¼ cup **agave nectar**
2 teaspoons **vanilla extract**
1 **vanilla bean**, seeds scraped out
1½ cups **coconut oil**, melted
2 tablespoons **fresh orange or clementine juice**
1 tablespoons **fresh lemon juice**
¼ cup **cashew nut butter**

1. With an immersion blender or in a food processor, combine the soy milk, ground almonds, agave, and vanilla extract. Blend until smooth.

2. Add the scraped seeds from the vanilla bean and keep the bean for another use.

3. Combine the melted coconut oil with the orange juice and lemon juice and add to the mixture gradually, blending until smooth. Add the cashew nut butter and again blend until smooth.

4. Chill overnight before using so that the coconut oil solidifies.

TIPS

✤ For pink frosting, replace ⅔ cup of the soy milk with ⅔ cup of pureed, strained raspberries or strawberries.

✤ You can play with other natural colors and flavors, as with Royal Icing (see page 189).

✤ If you can't do soy, substitute rice milk for the soy milk. The texture is not quite as smooth but the taste is great.

Better Carrot Cake

A beautiful carrot cake made without any dairy, wheat, gluten, soy or sugar. Baking with the ingredients below takes some getting used to—the batter will have a different consistency from a traditional wheat-based cake—but the results are worth the effort. Coconut oil and boiling water make the cake very moist. The rice flour gives the cake a fine texture and the spices and mandarin oil impart a unique flavor.

Serves: 8–10
Preparation time: 30 minutes
Cooking time: 45 minutes
♥ ✓ WF GF DF V

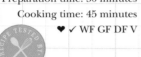

4 **carrots**, peeled and grated
½ small **apple** or ⅓ small **sweet potato**, grated
½ cup **dry unsweetened shredded coconut**
¼ cup **coconut oil**, melted
¼ cup **sunflower oil**
½ cup **agave nectar**
1½ teaspoons **yacon syrup** (optional)
2 teaspoons **vanilla extract**
½ cup **chickpea (besan) flour** or ⅔ cup **corn flour**
1 cup plus 2 tablespoons **gluten-free all-purpose flour**
1 teaspoon **xanthan gum**
1 teaspoon **gluten-free baking soda**
½ teaspoon **sea salt**
1½ teaspoons **ground cinnamon**
1 teaspoon **ground ginger**
¾ cup **hot water**
½ teaspoon **mandarin, lemon** or **orange extract**
1 quantity **Vegan Vanilla Frosting** (see page 97)

1. Heat the oven to 325°F. Butter a 9 inch loaf pan and line it with parchment paper.

2. Combine the carrots, apple or sweet potato, coconut, coconut oil, sunflower oil, agave, yacon syrup, and vanilla in a bowl and set aside.

3. Combine the dry ingredients in a second bowl and beat together to evenly distribute them. Beat in the carrot mixture.

4. Gradually pour in the hot water and citrus extract and mix to a smooth batter. Pour into the prepared pan.

5. Bake in the oven for about 40–45 minutes, or until a toothpick inserted into the center comes out clean. Turn out of the loaf pan and let cool completely. Ice with vanilla frosting.

TIPS

❖ Because there is no gluten in this recipe, the cake batter will look different from the ones you are used to. The xanthan gum works as a binding agent to hold it all together, so make sure you don't leave it out. If you have trouble finding it, you might find a gluten-free flour mix that contains the ingredient already.

Zucchini Bread

This sweet, dark bread is a staple here, enjoyed in the afternoon with a cup of coffee or tea. However, it is called courgette bread in England. The cinnamon works very well with the zucchini, and it's a great alternative to banana bread.

Be careful when shredding the zucchini, and use a grater with big holes.

Serves: 8–10
Preparation time: 20 minutes
Cooking time: 50 minutes
V

1¾ sticks **butter**, plus a little extra for greasing the tin
1 cup firmly packed **dark brown sugar**
3 **free-range eggs**
1 medium **zucchini**, washed and shredded (skin on)
1 ⅔ cups **all-purpose flour**
1 teaspoon **baking powder**
a pinch of **salt**
½ teaspoon **cinnamon**

1. Butter a 9 inch loaf pan and line it with parchment paper. Heat the oven to 340°F.

2. Melt the butter in a small saucepan. Put the brown sugar into a large bowl and beat in the eggs. Pour the melted butter into this in a steady stream until well mixed in. Stir in the grated zucchini.

3. Put the all-purpose flour, baking powder, salt, and cinnamon into another bowl and stir them together.

4. Add the wet ingredients to the dry ingredients and mix just until incorporated. Pour into the prepared loaf pan and bake for 40–50 minutes, or until springy and a toothpick inserted in the center comes out clean. Let cool in the pan.

VIOLET Coconut Macaroons

There is a sublime crispy gooiness to these maceroons that makes them like nothing else on earth. Warning: They are very addictive. Violet is the name of Claire's bakery and store on Wilton Way and her stall at Broadway Market, both in Hackney, London.

Makes: 12
Preparation time: 5 minutes
Cooking time: 15 minutes
❤ WF GF DF

3 **free-range egg whites**
¾ cup **superfine sugar**
2 teaspoons **honey**
2 cups **dry, unsweetened shredded coconut**
½ teaspoon **vanilla extract**

My friendship with Henry and Mima was ignited by their love of these macaroons, as they returned time and time again to my market stall to buy them.

CLAIRE

1. Heat the oven to 300°F. Line a baking sheet with parchment paper.

2. Combine the egg whites, sugar, salt, honey, and coconut in a large saucepan over medium heat.

3. Stir the mixture continuously until everything is dissolved and it just begins to scorch on the bottom.

4. Remove the saucepan from the heat and stir in the vanilla extract.

5. Let the mixture cool completely, then use an ice cream scoop (about ¼ cup) to scoop out 12 even macaroons, and place them on the baking sheet.

6. Bake in the oven for about 10–15 minutes, or until golden and set. Let the macaroons cool completely before peeling off the paper.

TIPS

+ The key to getting these macaroons just right is to stir the ingredients in the pan until they begin to dry out.

+ The vanilla extract isn't essential.

Leon Pecan Pie

A simple, rich, gluten-free pecan tart that has become a favorite in the restaurants. Baked by Craig Barton, one of our favorite bakers.

Serves: 8–10
Preparation time: 50 minutes
Cooking time:1 hour 10 minutes
WF GF V

4 tablespoons **butter**
1 cup **light corn syrup**
2 tablespoons **superfine sugar**
1 teaspoon **cornflour**
2 large free-range **eggs**
2 cups **pecan halves**

For the pastry dough:
1¼ sticks **butter**
½ cup **superfine sugar**
1 **free-range egg**, plus 1 **yolk**
2 cups plus 2 tablespoons **gluten-free all-purpose flour**

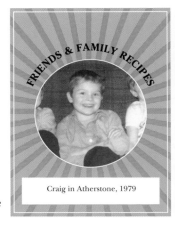

FRIENDS & FAMILY RECIPES

Craig in Atherstone, 1979

1. First make the dough by creaming together the butter and sugar with a wooden spoon or in a freestanding electric mixer until smooth.

2. Add the egg and egg yolk and mix until fully incorporated. Add the flour and quickly bring it together in a ball. Wrap the pastry in plastic wrap and refrigerate for at least 30 minutes.

3. Butter a 9–10 inch fluted tart pan. Roll the dough out on a floured surface to about ⅛ inch thick and line your tart pan with it. Trim the edges and chill in the refrigerator for 30 minutes. Meanwhile, heat the oven to 325°F.

4. Line the chilled pastry shell with parchment paper, and fill it with pie weights or dried beans to stop it from shrinking while it's being baked. Bake in the oven for 20 minutes, then remove the weights and paper. Return to the oven and bake for another 5 minutes. The pastry should be a nice blonde color. Set aside to cool.

5. Put the butter and corn syrup into a medium saucepan over a low heat. When it becomes runny, remove it from the heat and beat in the sugar.

6. In a small bowl, beat the cornstarch and eggs until smooth, then add to the saucepan.

7. Fill the baked pastry with the pecan halves. Pour the corn syrup mixture on top and fill it up to just below the edge of the shell. Put into the oven, being careful not to spill any liquid over the sides, because this might make it difficult to remove it from the pan once it's baked.

8. Bake for about 40 minutes, or until the tart is a dark golden color and has slightly risen in the middle. Take out of the oven and let cool in the pan.

TIPS

❖ Serve cold, or warm with Vanilla Ice Cream (see page 159).

Pecan Pie

Sweet and sticky and treacly and nutty

Petra's Honey Bread

A sweet, soft, wonderfully delicious quick bread. Dangerously addictive with a thick topping of butter.

Makes: 1 small loaf
Preparation time: 15 minutes
Cooking time: 1 hour
DF

1¾ cups **all-purpose flour**
⅔ cup **superfine sugar**
½ cup **honey**
1 cup **hot water**
1 teaspoon **baking of soda**
zest of 1 **lemon**

1. Heat the oven to 325°F. Butter a an 8½ inch loaf pan, and line it with parchment paper.

2. Mix together the flour and sugar in a large bowl.

3. In a small saucepan, melt together the honey and the water.

4. Sprinkle the baking soda over the water mixture and stir. Pour this over the dry ingredients and mix just until incorporated.

5. Turn the mixture into the prepared pan and bake in the oven for 50–60 minutes.

6. Remove from the pan and let cool, then serve thinly sliced, with butter.

TIPS

✤ You could brush the top of the warm bread with honey for a nice sticky finish.

✤ Try replacing the lemon zest with orange or clementine zest.

My mother-in-law, Petra, is the evil genius of baking. Whenever we go to her house she plies us with homemade sweet treats: everything from caramel shortbread to fresh drop-scones, folded up warm in white damask napkins. This honey bread is one of her master strokes. Elegantly arranged in thin slices, it has a subtle flavor that demands a second helping. Next thing you know you've eaten the lot.

HENRY

Good Scones

These scones are made with lots of alternative ingredients that make them healthier. But we like the idea of eating them with clotted cream anyway.

Makes: 12
Preparation time: 25 minutes
Cooking time: 25 minutes
♥ ✓ DF V

¾ cup **gluten-free all-purpose flour**
1 cup **white spelt flour**
3 teaspoons **gluten-free baking powder**
a large pinch of **salt**
¼ cup **coconut oil**, melted, or **sunflower oil**
2 tablespoons **maple syrup**
1 tablespoon **vanilla extract**
⅓ cup **hot water**
3 tablspoons **rice milk**
clotted cream or **crème fraîche**
    and **Fresh Strawberry Jam** (see page 226), to serve

1. Measure all the dry ingredients into a large bowl. In a small saucepan, melt the coconut oil and let it cool slightly. Pour the oil over the dry ingredients and toss together with a fork.

2. Mix the remaining ingredients except the cream and jam into the dry ingredients just until combined. Don't overwork it.

3. Let the dough rest for 10 minutes. Meanwhile line a baking sheet with parchment paper, and heat the oven to 350°F.

4. Roll out the dough ½–¾ inch thick. Use a cookie cutter or a glass to cut out circles.

5. Place the scones on the baking sheet and bake in the oven for 20–25 minutes.

6. When they are ready and firm to the touch, take them out of the oven and place on a cooling rack. Cool completely before splitting open and filling with cream and jam.

TIPS

You could make the scones wheat free by omitting the spelt flour and using either more of the gluten-free all-purpose flour or substituting chickpea (besan) flour for the spelt.

DESSERTS

FRUIT

Britain's climate and location provides the country with a wonderful array of fruit from spring (rhubarb), through peak summer (berries, plums), and into fall (quinces, pears, apples). Then, just when the cupboard is almost bare, the Spanish citrus fruits of midwinter come sailing to their rescue.

Most traditional English desserts feature one of these fruits in combination with flour, sugar, and dairy. Delicious, but not always nutritious. The recipes that follow contain a few comforting Brtish favorites alongside some healthier alternatives.

The thing to remember with fruit is that it is eminently substitutable. Like the manager of a fantasy football team, once you have mastered the broad shape of a dish, you can continually reinvent it by playing with another fruit.

GROWN AND PACKED BY

LEON

Roasted Peaches

Sometimes the best things are the simplest. Make sure you get the best peaches you can afford.

Serves: 4
Preparation time: 5 minutes
Cooking time: 15 minutes
WF GF (DF V if not using cream)

4 ripe **white** or **yellow peaches**
½ cup **white wine**
½ cup **superfine sugar**
heavy cream, to serve

1. Heat the oven to 350°F.

2. Halve the peaches and remove the pits. Arrange the peach halves in a roasting pan, cut side up. Add the white wine and sprinkle the superfine sugar over the top.

3. Bake in the oven for 12–15 minutes, until the fruit is bubbly and a little golden on the edges.

TIPS

❖ When the peaches come out of the oven, they will bubble as they start to cool down. Arrange them on small plates and pass around the cream.

❖ Use ripe delicious peaches. If they are underripe, no amount of cooking will be able to save them.

GEORGIA TAKING PICTURES OF BANANAS IN THE STREET

BBQ Chocolate Bananas

After the burgers and sausages have been made and the BBQ is cooling down, it is time to throw these babies on the grill. Easy and fun summer BBQ fare for the kids.

Serves: 6
Preparation time: 2 minutes
Cooking time: 10 minutes
✓ WF GF V

6 **bananas** in their skins
6 bars of your favorite **chocolate**, broken into pieces

1. Make a cut in the bananas from the stem to the opposite end through the peel and half way through the fruit.

2. Push in pieces of chocolate and place the bananas on the grill.

3. Cook until the chocolate starts to melt. The skins will blacken and not look very nice, but don't worry.

4. Serve.

 TIPS

❖ If you happen to have a little caramel sauce lingering in the refrigerator it would be delicious drizzled over these.

❖ Sprinkle with a little flaky sea salt for wonderful texture and flavor.

❖ You can serve them as they are in their skins, or carefully slip them out of the skins onto a plate and serve with a dollop of lightly whipped cream.

Baked Apples

Baked apples are easy and perfect for a chilly fall night. They deserve to be more fashionable than they are.

Serves: 4
Preparation time: 15 minutes
Cooking time: approx. 1 hour
♥ ✓ DF V
(WF GF if you use gluten-free bread)

4 medium **apples**, such as Cox's or Braeburn
1 slice of stale **bread**, white or gluten-free
½ cup homemade or other good-quality **mincemeat**
a pinch of **sea salt**

1. Heat the oven to 350°F. Line a baking sheet with parchment paper.

2. Dig out the cores of the apples without going all the way through to the bottom, then place them on individual squares of aluminum foil, big enough to wrap the apples, on the paper-lined baking sheet.

3. Tear the bread into pea-size pieces and mix with the mincemeat and salt. Pack the bread mixture into the apples. Bring the foil up and wrap it loosely around them, then bake in the oven for 45 minutes to an hour, until tender.

TIPS

✤ Serve with custard (see page 34) or heavy cream.

✤ Instead of mincemeat, the following work well as toppings: • Raspberries, brown sugar, and bread crumbs, served with vanilla ice cream. • Apricots, golden raisins, and sour cherries, in red wine and sugar, drizzled with butter, and served with heavy cream.

Pineapple Upside Down Cake

A carnival cake. Full of life. Full of flavor. A little bit kitsch. But deeply satisfying.

Serves: 6
Preparation time: 25 minutes
Cooking time: 40 minutes
V

125g very soft **unsalted butter**
scant 1 cup **superfine sugar**
2 **free-range eggs**
1 teaspoon **vanilla extract**
1 teaspoon **salt**
½ cup **whole milk**
1⅔ cups **all-purpose flour**
2 teaspoon **baking powder**
½ a **pineapple**, skin and core
    removed and cut into rings
For the caramel
1⅛ stick **unsalted butter**
⅔ cup firmly packed **light
    brown sugar**

1. Heat the oven to 340°F.

2. First make the caramel. Put the butter and brown sugar in the bottom of a deep 8 inch cake pan and place the pan directly over low heat on the stove. Stir continuously until the butter-sugar mixture comes together and bubbles. Set aside to cool.

3. Cream the butter and superfine sugar until light and fluffy. Add the eggs, one at a time and mix until incorporated. Add the vanilla and salt. Add half the milk and mix.

4. Sift together the flour and baking powder and add half to the mixture. Add the remaining milk and finally the rest of the flour.

5. Now that the caramel in the pan has cooled, cover it with the pineapple rings. Over that, pour the cake batter and smooth the surface. Bake in the oven for about 40 minutes. The top should spring back when cooked.

6. Let the cake sit in the pan for about 15 minutes before running a knife around the edge and inverting it onto a serving plate. If it is too hot, it can fall apart.

TIPS

❖ If the cake sticks, you can either pop it back in the oven to melt the caramel a little, or place the cake pan directly on the heat of the stove for a minute (no longer, or it could burn), which will melt the caramel and help release the cake.

❖ You could substitute white spelt flour here, which would work very nicely. However, this is not a great place for gluten-free flour. The heavy fruit and caramel needs a stronger sponge than a gluten-free version could provide.

❖ You can use canned pineapple.

Tarte Tatin

Crisp pastry and warm, soft caramelized apples in a pool of cream.

Serves: 8
Preparation time: 35 minutes
Cooking time: 40 minutes
V

9oz frozen **puff pastry**
flour, for rolling
4–6 medium **apples** (Cox's and Granny
    Smiths are good)
juice of ½ a **lemon**
2 tablespoons **unsalted butter**
⅓ cup **superfine sugar**
light cream, to serve

1. Heat the oven to 400°F. Line a baking sheet with parchment paper.

2. On a lightly floured surface, roll the pastry into a 12 inch circle. Use a sharp knife to carefully trim the edge, making as perfect a circle as you can without losing too much of the diameter. Place the pastry circle carefully on the lined baking sheet. Place it in the freezer if it will fit; if not, place it in the refrigerator.

3. Peel, quarter and core the apples and coat in lemon juice to stop them turning brown.

4. Place a medium oven-proof skillet on medium heat and melt the butter until it foams. Add the sugar and let it to dissolve. Turn up the heat and continue to cook until the sugar just starts to caramelize (turns light brown). Remove from the heat. The caramel will continue to darken as it cools, so remove it from the heat well before it reaches a dark caramel.

5. Arrange the apples tightly in the skillet in 2 layers.

6. Place the chilled circle of pastry over the top of the skillet and tuck the edges down inside. Pierce the pastry with a knife to let steam escape during baking.

7. Place the skillet in the oven and bake for about 30 minutes, or until the pastry is golden and the juices are bubbling at the sides. Remove from the oven and let the tart rest for 5 minutes.

8. Run a small knife around the edge of the skillet to release the tart. Place a serving plate slightly larger than the skillet over the tart, and quickly and carefully flip the tart over onto the plate. Drizzle any juices over the tart, then serve hot and eat with plenty of cream.

 TIPS

❖ If you are unsure about when to stop cooking the caramel, you can take it as dark as you like it and then stop the cooking process by dunking the bottom of the pan in a sink full of ice-cold water. This will stop the cooking so that the caramel does not burn.

❖ Try swapping the apples for pears or quinces.

Key Lime Pie

Key limes come from the Florida Keys (hence the name) and tend to be smaller and sweeter than conventional limes. If you can't get to Florida for your groceries, don't worry—the flavor will still be wonderful.

Serves: 6–8
Preparation time: 20 minutes
Cooking time: 35 minutes

V

1¾ cups **crushed Graham crackers**

6 tablespoons **unsalted butter,** melted

1 x (14oz) can **sweetened condensed milk**

4 **large free-range egg yolks**

1 tablespoon **lime zest,** plus extra for garnish (about 3 limes)

½ cup freshly squeezed **lime juice** (about 6 limes)

1½ cups **heavy cream,** chilled

1. Heat the oven to 350°F.

2. Combine the crushed Graham crackers and melted butter in a medium bowl and mix well. Press the mixture into a 9 inch pie plate and bake in the oven until lightly browned. This will take about 12–15 minutes. Remove from the oven and transfer to a wire rack until completely cooled.

3. Lower the oven to 325°F.

4. In a medium bowl, gently beat together the condensed milk, egg yolks, lime zest, and lime juice. Pour into the prepared, cooled shell.

5. Return the pie to the oven and bake until the center is set but still quivers when the plate is nudged. This should take 15–20 minutes.

6. Let the pie cool completely in the plate on top of a wire rack.

7. Once the pie has cooled, place it in the refrigerator to chill until ready to serve.

8. Before serving, lightly whip the cream into soft peaks. Spread the cream over the chilled pie.

9. Garnish with a little more lime zest.

TIPS

❖ To crush the Graham crackers, simply put them into a thick plastic bag and smash them with a rolling pin.

Jossy's Jeweled Rhubarb & Mango

This is a simple but sublime combination, which also looks beautiful. The appearance of the deep yellow mango with the clear pink rhubarb, and the combination of their contrasting flavors, is wonderful.

Serves: 4
Preparation time: 20 minutes
Cooking time: 1 hour
♥ WF GF DF V

1lb **early forced thin-stalked champagne rhubarb**
½ inch piece of **fresh ginger**
2 or 3 **star anise**
⅔ cup **cranberry juice**
juice of 2 **limes**
¼ cup **superfine sugar**
1 large or 2 small ripe **mangoes**
a few **mint leaves** to decorate

1. Heat the oven to 340°F.

2. Slice the rhubarb across on the diagonal into 2 inch pieces. Peel the ginger, cut it in half, and slice into small, very thin pieces.

3. Arrange the rhubarb, ginger and star anise in a wide ovenproof tart pan. Put the cranberry juice, lime juice, and sugar into a saucepan and bring to a boil, stirring until the sugar has dissolved. Boil fiercely for 2 minutes, then pour over the rhubarb.

4. Cover the dish tightly with aluminum foil and put it on the center shelf of the oven for about 1 hour, until the rhubarb is very soft. Remove from the oven, take off the foil and let cool completely.

5. Cut open the mangoes and cut the flesh off the pit, then skin them and slice into thin strips. Arrange the mango strips among the rhubarb, with the star anise dotted on top, then chill. Before serving, decorate with mint leaves.

Blueberry Cheesecake

A rich, creamy cheesecake cut by a sharper fruit topping. Luxurious.

Serves: 8–10
Preparation time: 20 minutes
Cooking time: 45 minutes–1 hour

1 cup **crushed Graham crackers**
1 cup **crushed gingersnaps**
6 tablespoons **unsalted butter**
2⅓ cups **cream cheese**
⅔ cup **superfine sugar**
2 teaspoons **lemon juice**
seeds from 1 **vanilla bean**
1 cup **crème fraîche** or **sour cream**
½ cup **Greek yogurt**
3 **extra large free-range eggs**

For the blueberry topping
2 small pints of **blueberries**
2 teaspoons **cornstarch**
3 tablespoons **water**

There is a tradition at Leon that if the team at one of the restaurants does something special, we bake them a cake. I baked this one for Remi and his team at our Cannon Street branch after they posted record sales. Putting the gingersnaps in the crust is a trick I learned from my mom. I figured they would go well with the blueberries.

HENRY

1. Heat the oven to 325°F.

2. Put the crushed Graham crackers and gingersnaps into a bowl. Melt the butter and pour it over the cookie crumbs, stirring to completely coat them.

3. Press the cookie mixture into the bottom of a deep 8 inch springform or loose-bottom cake pan, then put it into the refrigerator until firm.

4. Beat together the cream cheese, sugar, lemon juice, and vanilla seeds until creamy. Mix in the crème fraîche and yogurt, then the eggs, and beat until smooth.

5. Spoon the filling over the chilled cookie crust. Smooth over the top and bake in the oven for 45 minutes, or until the filling has set (it may need another 10 minutes).

6. Place the pan on a wire rack to cool completely, then run a small paring knife around the inside of the pan to help release the cheesecake from the pan.

7. Toss the blueberries in the cornstarch and put them in a small saucepan with the water. Heat while stirring until the blueberries are bubbling and start to break up. Let cool then spoon over the top of the cheesecake.

TIPS

❖ Cherries are always welcome on a cheesecake, as are cranberries. Add a teaspoon of almond extract for the cherry version, and finely grated orange zest with the cranberry version.

Poached Pears

Pears are such an everyday fruit that it's easy to overlook their beauty. Poaching them in wine is the simplest way to turn this Eliza Doolittle into an elegant society lady.

Serves: 6
Preparation time: 10 minutes
Cooking time: approx. 20 minutes
♥ WF GF DF V

2 bottles of **white wine**
zest of 1 **lemon**
1 **vanilla bean**, split and the seeds scraped
1½ cups **caster sugar**
1¼ cups **water**
6 firm but ripe **pears**

1. Put all the ingredients except the pears into a sauce pan large enough to hold all the pears and heat to dissolve the sugar, stirring occasionally.

2. Peel the pears and drop them into the poaching liquid.

3. Let the liquid come to a very light simmer, with bubbles the size of tiny shrimp eyes.

4. Cook until the pears are tender (about 20–30 minutes, depending on ripeness).

5. Serve with cream, Sabayon (see below), or Quick Custard (see page 34).

TIPS

❖ Poach the pears in red wine instead of white, but change the lemon zest to orange zest, and the vanilla to a cinnamon stick. Or cut the recipe in half and make three red and three white wine pears.

❖ Save the poaching liquid and reduce it a little. This makes a wonderful sauce to drizzle over ice cream or a simple cake such as Clementine Cornmeal Cake (page 89).

Sabayon

Sabayon, or zabaglione in Italian, is a perfect accompaniment to any poached fruit, but equally good with just a crispy sweet cookie.

Serves: 4–6
Preparation time: 5 minutes
Cooking time: 35 minutes
WF GF V

⅓ cup **Muscat, Sauternes** or **Marsala**
1 tablespoon **superfine sugar**
4 **free-range egg yolks**
1 cup h**eavy cream**

1. Place the wine in a small saucepan on the stove and cook gently until it has reduced by half.

2. Using an electric handheld mixer, beat the caster sugar and egg yolks to thick ribbons.

3. In a steady stream, pour the hot reduced wine directly into the egg yolk mixture. Continue to whisk until cool to touch—it must be completely cool before you add the cream, otherwise the cream will melt and you will lose all the volume.

4. Lightly whip the cream, then fold it gently through the mixture.

Fools & Jellies

The simplest way to show off fruit in a dessert is either to set it into a "jelly" or gelatin, or fold it into whipped cream to make a "fool". They are both very traditional English puddings.

Gooseberry Fool

Henry has a small, slightly sad gooseberry bush at the bottom of his garden that produces about enough gooseberries each year to make one helping of fool. Here is the recipe.

Serves: 6
Preparation time: 10 minutes
Cooking time: 10 minutes
WF GF V

2½ cups **gooseberries**
a couple of tablespoons of **water**
⅓ cup **superfine sugar**
2 cups **heavy cream**

1. Put the gooseberries and water into a pan over a medium heat and cook for 10 minutes, until the fruit is very soft.

2. Blitz briefly in a food processor with the sugar, checking for sweetness. Pass through a biggish sieve to get rid of the pips.

3. Whip the cream into soft peaks and loosely fold in the gooseberries so that there are still streaks of cream.

4. Serve in a large bowl, or in cold glasses if you want to be fancy.

TIPS

✤ Acidic fruits are best for fools if you want to substitute something else for the gooseberries. Try rhubarb, plums, or raspberries.

Blood Orange & White Wine Gelatin

There is something about the limpid tremble of a lightly set jelly that is devilishly alluring. This one is based on a recipe from Richard Olney's 1970 classic *The French Menu Cookbook*. His recipe includes instructions on how to make the gelatin by boiling calves' feet. Thankfully we can now buy perfectly good gelatin (from animal sources or vegetarian) in pristine transparent sheets.

Serves: 6
Preparation time: 10 minutes
Cooking time: 10 minutes
♥ WF GF DF
(V if you use vegetarian gelatine)

⅔ cup **sweet white wine** (Muscat or Baumes de Venise)
¼ cup **superfine sugar**
1 stick of **cinnamon**
2 cups fresh **blood orange juice** (5 or 6 oranges)
4 sheets of **gelatin** (about 4 teaspoons)

1. Put the wine into a saucepan with the sugar, the cinnamon stick and ⅔ cup of the orange juice. Bring to a boil, then remove from the heat and remove the cinnamon. Melt the gelatin into the juice (following the package directions).

2. Pour the rest of the orange juice into a bowl and pour in the liquid from the pan. Stir thoroughly, then pour into your mold. Let cool, then put into the refrigerator until set.

3. To turn out, loosen the edges of the gelatin gently with your fingers. Dip the mold into a bowl of hot water for 1–2 seconds, place a plate on top, then invert the mold and shake. Serve with light cream or heavy cream.

TIPS

✚ Richard Olney uses orange and lemon juice instead of blood orange juice. You can experiment with all kinds of liquids: white wines, pomegranate juice, grapefruit juice and lime juice are all good.

✚ Try flavoring the gelatin with herbs and spices— rosemary with orange, for example, or cardamom with coconut milk.

✚ We prefer a lighter set. Use less gelatin where you can get away with it.

✚ Try putting whole fruit inside your gelatin (grapes, peach slices, strawberries, raspberries, etc). You can make the fruit float if you first set a layer of gelatin, then add the fruit, followed by the rest of the gelatin.

✚ Some fruits have enzymes that digest gelatin, which will make it hard to set. These include: figs, kiwis, mango, melon, papaya, peach, pineapple, and ginger.

COBBLERS, CRISPS & CRUMBLES

These are all ways to add a little sweet crunch to a dish of stewed fruit. The cobbler has small, flat biscuits of pastry, like cobblestones, baked on top. The British crumble is covered completely with a … well, crumbly top. Our crisps are like a crumble, but with a much thinner crispy layer. The good news is that all three form gooey caramelized bits around the side of the dish.

Strawberry & Blueberry Cobbler

Cobblers are the perfect summer dessert. (In fact, they make a damned good summer Sunday breakfast.) The cobbler topping is like a biscuit and melts into the jammy fruit. Serve this one with thick cream.

Serves: 6
Preparation time: 15 minutes
Cooking time: 40 minutes
WF GF V

8oz **blueberries**
1lb **strawberries**, hulled and quartered
¼ cup **superfine sugar**
¼ cup **cornstarch**
1½ cups **gluten-free all-purpose flour**
4 teaspoons **gluten-free baking powder**
a large pinch of **salt**
3½ tablespoons **unsalted butter**, cut into small cubes
⅔ cup **heavy cream**, plus extra to brush the topping

1. Heat the oven to 350°F.

2. Combine the berries, sugar and cornstarch and put into a deep 1–1½ quart baking dish.

3. Put the flour, baking powder, salt, and butter into a bowl and use the back of a fork or two knives to break up the chunks of butter into tiny pieces. Pour over the cream and mix until it all comes together.

4. Press the topping into a ball and place on a floured work surface. Let the mixture rest for 10 minutes. Then roll out to a ¾ inch thickness and cut out circles with a cookie cutter.

5. Lay the circles flat over the fruit, brush with extra cream, and place on a baking sheet to catch any drips.

6. Bake in the oven for 35–40 minutes, or until the fruit is bubbly and the topping is golden brown.

 TIPS

❖ You can also make this cobbler topping with regular all-purpose flour.

❖ Experiment with different fruits: peaches and nectarines work well, with a little added lemon zest and juice.

Dittisham Plum Crumble

Crumbles are all about getting the balance right between sweet and sour and soft and crisp. This makes a lovely conclusion to a simple summer supper.

Serves: 6
Preparation time: 15 minutes
Cooking time: 45 minutes
WF GF V

2½lb tart **plums**
¼ cup **superfine sugar**
3 tablespoons **gluten-free all-purpose flour**
1 tablespoon **sweet white wine**

For the crumble topping
¾ cup **gluten-free all-purpose flour**
1 cup **ground almonds**
½ cup **flaked almonds**
⅓ cup firmly packed **brown sugar**
a pinch of **sea salt**
¼ teaspoon **ground cinnamon**
1¼ sticks **unsalted butter**, cut into ¼ inch cubes

1. Heat the oven to 350°F.

2. Halve and pit the plums and place in a bowl. Toss with the sugar, flour, and wine and put into a deep 9–10 inch square baking dish.

3. Put all the crumble topping ingredients into a bowl and use the back of a fork or two knives to break up the chunks of butter into tiny pieces.

4. Scatter the topping lightly over the fruit and place in the oven.

5. Bake for 40–45 minutes, or until the fruit is bubbly and the topping is golden.

TIPS

❖ Almonds and plums go nicely together here, but you could substitute hazelnuts and blueberries, or walnuts and apples.

The plums of Dittisham in Devon, have long been famous for their tart and deep-fruity flavor. I developed this recipe when my husband and I went for a magical vacation in Dittisham with Henry's family. During the day, we were sailing and swimming and sunning ourselves; by the evening, everyone was ravenous. Henry's aunt brought us some plums from her yard, and we rustled up this crowd-pleasing crumble.

CLAIRE

Apple Crisp

A very easy dessert, and another great way to turn your stale bread into something delicious and sumptuous.

Serves: 6
Preparation time: 10 minutes
Cooking time: 35 minutes
V (WF GF if you use gluten-free bread)

3¼lb **apples**, peeled, quartered, and cored

juice of 1 **lemon**

⅓ cup **superfine sugar**, plus an extra 2 tablespoons for sprinkling

¼ teaspoon **ground cinnamon**

8 sheets **stale**, **crusty white bread**, crusts removed and torn into pieces

¼lb **salted butter**, melted

1. Heat the oven to 350°F.

2. Combine the apples, lemon juice, sugar, and cinnamon and put into a deep 1–1½ quart baking dish.

3. In a bowl, toss the bread pieces in the melted butter and then arrange in a layer over the apples. Sprinkle sugar over the top and place on a baking sheet to catch any drips.

4. Bake in the oven for 30–35 minutes, or until the fruit is bubbly and the topping is golden.

(TIPS)

❖ Serve hot with cream.

❖ Try using pears instead of apples and add a splash of white wine.

❖ Don't use sourdough or levain bread because it will be too sour. Use plain, white bread or a French baguette, nice and stale.

MERIN

/m ˈra / *n.* a delicate confection the chief ingredients of which are pounded sugar and whites of eggs.

BAKING WITH MERINGUE CAN BE INTIMIDATING, BUT IT NEEDN'T BE WHEN YOU KNOW A FEW TRICKS AND YOU HAVE THE RIGHT TOOLS. AN ELECTRIC HANDHELD MIXER OR FREESTANDING MIXER IS ALWAYS GOING TO MAKE MERINGUE MAKING EASIER. MERINGUE CAN TAKE AN INCREDIBLE AMOUNT OF BEATING (UNLIKE CREAM) SO IT IS HARD TO OVERDO IT. USING A PINCH OF SALT OR A PINCH OF CREAM OF TARTAR CAN HELP TO STABILIZE THE WHITES AND KEEP THEM FROM "BREAKING".

GUES

WHITES ARE "BROKEN" WHEN THEY DEVELOP A SANDY TEXTURE AND DO NOT TURN GLOSSY. ADDING SUGAR GRADUALLY AT THE BEGINNING OF THE BEATING PROCESS IS A GOOD IDEA, TO STABILIZE. IF YOU ARE USING SUPERFINE SUGAR (AS OPPOSED TO GRANULATED SUGAR), THE SECOND HALF OF IT CAN GO IN ALL AT ONCE WITHOUT CAUSING ANY PROBLEMS. THE FINE TEXTURE OF SUPERFINE SUGAR MEANS IT DISSOLVES QUICKLY AND CAN BE INCORPORATED WITH NO PROBLEM.

Mont Blanc

Chestnuts are the unsung heroes of the winter table. Their subtle but rich flavor is enhanced when sweetened and combined with vanilla. This is one of the classic desserts—loved by the Italians and the French, named after their favorite mountain.

Serves: 6
Preparation time: 10 minutes
Cooking time: 2½ hours
WF GF V

For the meringue
3 **free-range egg whites**
¼ teaspoon **salt**
1 teaspoon **vanilla extract**
1 cup **superfine sugar**

For the filling
1 x (15½oz) can **sweetened chestnut puree**
1¼ cups **heavy cream**, lightly whipped

1. Preheat the oven to 250°F. Line 2 baking sheets with parchment paper.

2. Using an electric handheld mixer, beat the egg whites, salt, and vanilla on a high speed until soft peaks form.

3. Add half the sugar to the frothy egg whites. Beat until very stiff, then add the remaining sugar. Beat until smooth and glossy.

4. Make 6 large meringue circles about 1½ inches apart on the prepared baking sheets. Bake in the oven for about 2½ hours. Let cool on the baking sheet before peeling from the paper.

5. When ready to serve, spoon the chestnut puree over the meringues and top with lightly whipped cream.

TIPS

✦ Sweetened chestnut puree is available on the Internet. It is made from candied chestnuts and has a wonderful texture and translucence. If you can't find it already prepared, however, you have a number of options:

• Take an unsweetened chestnut puree and sweeten it to taste with confectioners' sugar and vanilla essence, whizzing it all up in a food processor. Add cream or ricotta cheese if you want a softer texture.

• Buy crystallized chestnuts (marrons glacés) and puree them with a little vanilla extract, but no sugar.

• Make the puree from scratch. Buy fresh chestnuts, make a cut in each shell, and boil them in water for about 10 minutes. Peel off the shells and skins and process the chestnuts in a food processor. Add just enough heavy cream to form a paste. Then add confectioners' sugar and vanilla extract to taste.

Baked Alaska

This is fun to make, easier than you would think, and will make your guests squeal with nostalgic delight.

Serves: 8
Preparation time: 15 minutes +
3 hours freezing time
Cooking time: 5 minutes

V 🍴

4 cups **vanilla** or **strawberry ice cream** (or any favourite flavor, store-bought, or see pages 157–9)

1 x **sponge cake layer**, 8 inches in diameter store-bought, or use ¼ recipe of Ben's Classic "Victoria Sponge", (see page 86)

4 **free-range egg whites**, at room temperature

¼ teaspoon **cream of tartar**

1 cup **superfine sugar**

Thomas Jefferson is thought to have invented a version of this dish, but most people seem to agree that the credit should go to the eighteenth-century American physicist Benjamin Thompson. It's a stunt pudding made possible by scientific thinking: the ice cream is insulated by the air trapped in the sponge and meringue. Every time I attempt it I don't think it's going to work, but it always does.

CLAIRE

1. Line an 8 inch diameter bowl with plastic wrap.

2. Take the ice cream of your choice (we have some wonderful recipes in this book, see pages 157–9, either way, you will want a slightly softened ice cream to press into your prepared bowl). Pack the ice cream into the bowl very tightly and cover with more plastic wrap. Place in the freezer for at least 3 hours.

3. Heat the oven to 425°F. Place the cake sponge on a baking tray lined with paper and set aside.

4. Put the egg whites into a large, clean bowl, and use an electric handheld mixer to beat them into soft peaks. Add the cream of tartar, then gradually add the sugar. Beat until super stiff and glossy.

5. Take the ice cream out of the freezer and discard the top layer of plastic wrap. Dunk the bottom of the bowl into a sink of hot water for a second. Invert the bowl over the sponge and use the plastic wrap to help coax the ice cream from the bowl. Discard the plastic wrap and immediately cover with the meringue. Use a knife to coax the meringue into peaks.

6. Bake in the oven for 5 minutes, until the peaks are golden.

7. Serve immediately!

TIPS

✦ Some say that using a Swiss meringue made with hot syrup (see steps 2–4 on page 157) will yield a stiffer Alaska that does not slide off the sides of the ice cream as you assemble it. We find that the real trick is to have very stiff meringue and very cold ice cream. A Swiss meringue is a lot more fussy, and the joy of this dessert is how easy it is, while being über-impressive.

Pavlova

There are hundreds of ways to dress a pavlova, but this is our favorite: simple and clean and drizzled with the sharp, juicy pulp of passion fruit. We like to serve it on individual meringues to make the recipients feel extra special.

Serves: 6
Preparation time: 20 minutes
Cooking time: 2 hours
WF GF V

3 **free-range egg whites**
¼ teaspoon **salt**
½ teaspoon **white wine vinegar**
½ teaspoon **pure vanilla extract**
1½ cups **superfine sugar**, plus an extra 2 tablespoons
1½ teaspoons **cornstarch**
3 tablespoons **raspberry jam**, to serve
1 cup **heavy cream**, lightly whipped, to serve
2 pints **strawberries**, to serve
3 **passion fruit**, to serve

1. Heat the oven to 250°F. Line a baking sheet with baking paper.

2. Using an electric handheld mixer, beat the egg whites, salt, vinegar, and vanilla on a high speed until soft peaks form.

3. Whisk 1 cup of sugar and the cornstarch together by hand and add half to the frothy egg whites. Use the electric handheld mixer to whip until very stiff, then add the remaining ½ cup of sugar. Beat until smooth and glossy.

4. Spoon 6 large swoops of the meringue onto your baking sheet, 1½ inches apart.

5. Bake in the oven for about 2 hours, then check the meringues. Remove from the oven when dry and firm. It should be possible to gently peel them off the paper. If they stick to the paper, they're not ready. Cool completely.

6. To assemble, place the meringues on a large serving plate or individual plates. Put a spoonful of raspberry jam on each and then a generous dollop of cream.

7. Cut and quarter the strawberries and toss with the 2 tablespoons of superfine sugar. Leave to macerate for a few minutes while you halve the passion fruits.

8. Stir the strawberries and divide between the pavlovas. Scoop out half a passion fruit onto each and serve.

The Australians and the New Zealanders still squabble about who created the pavlova, which was named after the Russian ballerina Anna Pavlova after she had toured the Antipodes in 1926 (the meringue is meant to look like a tutu). It is a moot point really, as desserts made from combining fruit, cream and meringue had been popular for ages – it is just that somehow this name stuck.

TIPS

❖ You can prepare the strawberries up to 2 hours in advance and keep them in the refrigerator to save time.

❖ The meringues can be made up to 5 days in advance and kept in an airtight container.

Chocolate

Chocolate is the Casanova of the culinary world. Nothing else inspires such lust; such swivel-eyed devotion. Women, especially, go weak at the knees for it. There are all kinds of scientific theories about why this should be. Chocolate contains hundreds of mood-altering chemicals, including theobromine—a mildly addictive stimulant also found in caffeine. In a small way, it gets you high.

Even if it didn't, chocolate would still be one of the world's most sensuous foods. Hard and melting, bitter and sweet, it's like having a romantic hero in your mouth. The following recipes are designed to make the most of chocolate's seductive qualities—these are desserts so irresistible that your guests will be swooning over them for years to come. You weren't going to make them just for yourself now, were you?

Leon Chocolate Mousse

This is a recipe from the first cookbook (one of the magnificent creations of Leon cofounder Allegra McEvedy). We included it here because it is a favorite in the restaurants and we know there are a lot of people who want to make it themselves.

Serves: 4
Preparation time: 25 minutes
Cooking time: none
✓ WF GF V

4oz **chocolate** (70% cocoa solids)
2 tablespoons **unsalted butter**
2 **free-range egg yolks**
1 shot of **dark espresso**
a drop of **orange oil** or very finely grated
    zest of ½ orange (optional)
3 **free-range egg whites**
1 tablespoon **fructose**

1. Melt the chocolate and butter until smooth in a large heatproof bowl in the microwave, or over a saucepan of simmering water, making sure the water does not touch the surface of the bowl.

2. Separately beat the egg yolks until nearly white and thick in consistency. Gently stir the whisked yolks into the butter and chocolate, then stir in the coffee and the orangey bit, if you are adding it.

3. Use an electric handheld mixer to whip the egg whites to soft peaks, then add the fructose and beat for another minute just to get that shine.

4. Beat a third of the egg white into the chocolate mixture until smooth, then add the next third more gently, and the last with the strokes of an angel.

5. Neither overmix nor leave white streaks, then divide the mousse into pretty things and leave in the refrigerator for an hour.

TIPS

❖ You can use Cointreau or Grand Marnier instead of orange oil or zest. Or you can omit the orange flavor altogether.

❖ If you don't have fructose, you can use 2 tablespoons of superfine sugar (you need more because fructose is slightly sweeter).

Warm Gooey Chocolate Cakes

One of those chocolate-oozing-out-of-the-middle desserts that is not nearly as hard to make as your awestruck guests will assume.

Serves: 6–8
Preparation time: 10 minutes
Cooking time: 7 minutes
WF GF V

1 tablespoon **superfine sugar**

6 tablespoons **unsalted butter**

5oz **dark chocolate**

a pinch of **salt**

⅓ cup **unsweetened cocoa powder**

2 **free-range egg whites**

1. Heat the oven to 400°F.

2. Butter individual mini molds and sprinkle each one with some superfine sugar.

3. Melt the butter, chocolate, and salt in a large heatproof bowl over simmering water. When all is melted, sift in the cocoa powder.

4. In a separate bowl, beat together the egg whites and sugar until soft peaks form. Combine with the melted chocolate by folding gently and trying not to knock out too much air.

5. Spoon the mixture into the molds and bake in the oven for just 7 minutes.

 TIPS

❖ Whatever you do, do not overbake these. They continue to bake slightly as they cool down, so take them out of the oven just before you think they are ready.

❖ Serve with cream and a splash of Cognac if you have some around.

❖ You could also make a whipped Chantilly cream by adding a small amount of sugar and vanilla extract to whipping cream.

Life by Chocolate Cake

This fudgy, flourless chocolate cake is SO rich, yet superlight, like a mousse. Once you have added it to your repertoire, you will make it again and again, not least because your friends and family will give you no choice. You have been warned.

Serves: 10–12
Preparation time: 20 minutes
Cooking time: 40 minutes
WF GF V

5 **free-range eggs**
1 cup firmly packed **soft light brown sugar**
½ cup **instant espresso**
12oz **semisweet chocolate**, broken into pieces
2¼ sticks **unsalted butter**, cut into small pieces
1 teaspoon **vanilla extract**
a pinch of **sea salt**

1. Heat the oven to 325°F. Butter a 9 inch cake pan, preferably not loose-bottom, and line the bottom and sides with parchment paper.

2. With an electric handheld mixer, beat the eggs and ½ cup of the sugar to voluminous peaks.

3. In a saucepan, dissolve the remaining sugar with the coffee over medium heat, then stir in the chocolate pieces and butter and remove from the heat.

4. Add the vanilla and salt to the saucepan and stir occasionally until everything is completely melted.

5. In a steady stream, pour the melted chocolate mixture into the beaten eggs and stir just until combined.

6. Pour into the prepared cake pan, then place in a deep roasting pan and pour enough hot water into the roasting pan to reach almost to the top of the cake pan.

7. Bake in the oven for 35–40 minutes. The cake should be set but not solid. Let cool in the pan.

 TIPS

❖ This cake tastes even more beautiful with a little dollop of crème fraîche.

Line the pan

Beat the eggs until they look like this

Butter, sugar, coffee, and chocolate

Fold it in slowly

Be careful not to overmix

Pour in the water

GRANITAS, SORBETS & ICE CREAMS

Many people feel that to make ice creams, they need an ice cream machine. However, while the machines are a lovely gadget, you don't need to invest in expensive hardware to make beautiful frozen desserts.

In this section we cover four techniques for making ice creams and the like. Two don't require a machine at all, while the other two are easier if you have one, but can be made without if you are prepared to put in the labor.

We have given one or two recipes for each technique and some suggestions for alternative flavors, so once you have mastered the basics, you can experiment merrily.

The techniques are:

GRANITA

The simplest of all of the frozen desserts. A flavored (cream-free) syrup is simply agitated throughout the freezing process with a whisk and forms lovely shards of ice as it freezes. The resulting dessert is crunchy, light, and refreshing. If you are planning a multicourse banquet (and who isn't?), an alcoholic, citrusy granita is a wonderful way to clear the palate between the appetizer and main course.

SORBET

Similar to a granita, but churned—either in a machine or by hand—so that it has a very light, snowy texture. A protein of some kind is usually added to a sorbet to give it that fuller texture. Gelatin, egg whites, or alcohol are usually used.

ICE CREAM

THE ITALIAN MERINGUE METHOD
Henry's mom, cookery writer Josceline Dimbleby, has never been one for kitchen gadgetry. She has, therefore, become an expert cheat at making ice cream. She has tried just about every method (her first book—*A Taste of Dreams*, published in 1976—included a remarkably tasty ice cream made from a package of Bird's Dream Topping), but her all-time favorite is the Italian meringue method.

This works by folding a meringue mixture into the whipped cream and fruit. You can then put it into the freezer without churning it: the air bubbles in the meringue prevent any large ice crystals from forming. You are left with a wonderfully smooth, creamy ice cream. This same method can be applied when using egg yolks and whipping them with sugar until they are voluminous and almost white. Richer but equally good.

ICE CREAM

THE TRADITIONAL CUSTARD METHOD
This is the classic method, in which egg yolk is used to make a rich custard base. It makes a dense, luxurious ice cream. You cannot simply leave it in the freezer, otherwise long, crunchy ice crystals will form. This is where an ice cream machine comes in useful. Otherwise, you'll need to freeze the mixture in a shallow, wide container, that will fit into your freezer. Every 30 minutes use a whisk to stir and break up the ice that has formed until it becomes a light ice cream.

Champagne Granita

A lovely, light way to end a meal. Or, if you are feeling extravagant, to serve as a palate cleanser between the appetizer and the main course (see picture on page 151, top).

Serves: 4–6
Preparation time: 10 minutes
Freezing time: 3–4 hours
♥ WF GF DF V

½ cup **superfine sugar**
1 cup **water**
1⅓ cups **Champagne**
(½ a bottle)
juice of 1 **lemon**

We originally wanted to do an absinthe granita, one that would make a party swing. Sadly, the stuff was so alcoholic that we couldn't get it to freeze, leaving us with a lethal, ice-cold absinthe syrup. Best to stick to Champagne really.

CLAIRE

1. Dissolve the sugar and water together in a saucepan over moderate heat. Stir in the Champagne. Add lemon juice to taste.

2. Freeze in a roasting pan or other container that is shallow and wide, but that will fit into your freezer. Every 30 minutes, use a whisk to stir and break up the ice that has formed, until all the liquid has turned into paper-thin ice shards.

TIPS

❖ You can play around with granitas as much as you want. Sharp rosé wine and fruit work well together, as do coffee, and vodka.

❖ Different alcohols also go well with different fruits. The alcohol can really bring out the flavor of a fruit, lifting it and making it more complex. Try Grand Marnier with orange, kirsch with cherries or pineapple. There are some wonderful small distilleries cropping up that are mixing fruits and alcohol. You can find pear, greengage, quince, and others. They are worth seeking out.

Quince Granita

A more scented, full-bodied granita, and a wonderful way to finish off a dinner on a cool evening (see picture on page 151, below left).

Serves: 6
Preparation time: 25 minutes
Cooking time: 2 hours
Freezing time: 5 hours
♥ WF GF DF V

1½ **quinces**
1½ cups **superfine sugar**
3 cups **water**
1 **vanilla bean**, split in half lengthwise
juice of ½ a **lemon**

1. Peel and quarter the quinces. Put the sugar, water, and vanilla bean into a saucepan and stir to dissolve the sugar. Bring to a boil.

2. Add the quinces and the lemon juice. Simmer for 1–2 hours, or until the quinces are tender when pierced and rosy in color.

3. Remove the quinces from the syrup and core them. Remove the vanilla bean.

4. Puree the quinces and syrup together, then add some water to adjust the consistency so it's less thick.

5. Freeze in a roasting pan or other container that is shallow and wide, but will fit into your freezer. Every 30 minutes, use a whisk to stir and break up the ice that has formed, until all the liquid has turned into paper-thin ice shards.

TIPS

❖ Quinces are thick and fluffy when pureed and lend themselves very well to being frozen. Be sure to cook them long enough so that they are tender.

❖ Add a teaspoon or two of honey to the puree as a variation. Honey and quince have an affinity for each other.

Clementine Granita

A light, fruity granita for winter refreshment (see picture on page 151, below right).

Serves: 4–6
Preparation time: 5 minutes
Cooking time: 10 minutes
Freezing time: 3–4 hours
♥ WF GF DF V

½ cup **water**
¼ cup **superfine sugar**
1¼ cups **clementine juice**, strained

1. Combine the water and sugar over low heat to make a syrup. Cool completely.

2. Stir in the strained clementine juice.

3. Freeze in a roasting pan or other container that is shallow and wide, but that will fit into your freezer. Every 30 minutes, use a whisk to stir and break up the ice that has formed, until all the liquid has turned into paper-thin ice shards.

TIPS

❖ Serve with grapefruit or orange sections, in pretty glass cups.

❖ It is also nice with a crisp, buttery cookie.

Apple Sorbet

We call this apple sorbet, but apple snow might be a better description. It is light and fluffy and pure as the driven … The egg white and gelatin add protein, which gives the sorbet its gorgeous texture.

Serves: 4–6
Preparation time: 25 minutes
Freezing time: up to 5 hours
❤ WF GF DF V

2 cups **apple cider**
¼ cup **superfine sugar**
1 teaspoon **powdered gelatin**
1 **free-range egg white**
a splash of **apple brandy** (optional)

1. Gently heat 1 cup of the apple cider with the sugar in a small saucepan.

2. In another saucepan, soften the gelatin with the remaining apple cider before heating it gently to dissolve. Once dissolved, combine the two liquids and pour into a container to cool. When cooled, place in the refrigerator until ready to freeze.

3. Beat the egg white to soft peaks and fold it into the chilled sorbet base. Add the apple brandy, if using, then pour into an ice cream machine and freeze according to the manufacturer's instructions.

TIPS

❖ Use a high-quality apple cider, or, even better, juice your own apples.

❖ Try substituting pear, peach, watermelon, or grape juice for the cider, or use apple juice. If they are sweet, you might need a squeeze of lemon to add some acidity.

Plum Parfait (aka Jossy's Damson Ice Cream)

Fluffy and creamy at the same time, this is an easy ice cream that does not require an ice cream machine.

Serves: 6–8
Preparation time: 10 minutes
Cooking time: 20 minutes
Freezing time: 5 hours minimum
WF GF V

¾–1lb **plums** or **damsons** (not too ripe)

juice of 1 **lemon**

¾ cup plus 2 tablespoons **superfine sugar**

2 extra-large **free-range egg whites**

a pinch of **salt**

1 cup **superfine sugar**

6 tablespoons strained **lemon juice**

1¼ cups **whipping cream**

2–3 tablespoons **plum** or other **fruit liqueur** (optional)

1. Cook the plums in advance: cut them in half, remove the pits, and put the fruit into a large saucepan with the lemon juice, and ¾ cup plus 2 tablespoons superfine sugar. Cover the pan and put over low heat, stirring often until the sugar has dissolved. Cook gently until mushy. Then put into a food processor, process to a rough puree and let stand until cold.

2. Now put the egg whites into a large, clean bowl with the salt and use an electric handheld mixer to beat until they begin to stand in soft peaks.

3. Put the remaining 1 cup of superfine sugar into a saucepan with the lemon juice and stir over low heat until dissolved. Then increase the heat and boil fiercely, without stirring, for 3 minutes.

4. Pour the syrup immediately onto the beaten egg whites from above in a thin stream, beating all the time with the electric handheld mixer until the mixture is thick and looks like uncooked meringue.

5. In a separate bowl, beat the cream until thick but not stiff. Then, using a metal spoon, gently but thoroughly fold the cream into the egg white mixture, followed by the plum puree. If you are using fruit liqueur, gradually stir it in.

6. Finally, turn the mixture into a serving bowl—glass looks pretty, but make sure it's freezer-proof—and freeze for at least 5 hours before eating.

TIPS

❖ Add a blob of crème fraîche on top of the parfait before serving.

❖ Try making this with pureed berries or mango for other delicious ice cream flavors.

This is a dish that my mom used to make for us every summer in Dittisham in Devon. The Dittisham Ploughman plum is found only in this village, and is thought to have been brought over here by German monks. These plums are particularly good for desserts, because they have great acidity. If yours are sweeter, add more lemon juice.

HENRY

Ice Cream Base

The base for almost all ice creams. Once you have mastered this, you can experiment by adding fruit purees, dried fruits, booze, candied nuts, or even caramelized days-old bread crumbs. This base is made with both heavy cream and whole milk, making it a little lighter than usual and consequently a better vehicle for other flavors.

Makes: about 3¾ cups
Preparation time: 30 minutes
Freezing time: up to 5 hours
WF GF V

5 **free-range egg yolks**
1¼ cups **double cream**
1¼ cups **whole milk**
1 cup **superfine sugar**

1. Make sure the eggs are at room temperature. Crack them into a large bowl and beat them briefly to break up the yolks.

2. Pour the cream into a plastic container that will hold all the ingredients and also fit into your refrigerator. Place a fine strainer over this and then set aside.

3. Put the milk and superfine sugar into a small saucepan. Bring to just under a boil, stirring to make sure the sugar dissolves.

4. Pour the hot milk slowly into the eggs, beating as you work.

5. Pour the milk-egg mixture back into the pan and place back on the stove. Stir continuously with a wooden spoon or a heatproof plastic spatula. It is ready when you can swipe a finger through the custard and leave a trail on the back of a spoon. This should happen quite quickly.

6. Immediately, pour the custard through the fine strainer into the reserved cream. Straining removes any bits of cooked egg, and if you are flavoring the custard with vanilla or coffee beans, for example, they will be strained out.

7. Give the ice cream base a good stir and taste. If it needs a pinch of salt or a teaspoon of vanilla extract or brandy, now is a good time to add it.

8. Chill the base until cold (it's a good idea to start the day before you're ready to freeze it, or early in the morning). Pour into an ice cream machine and freeze, according to the manufacturer's instructions.

❖ When tasting your ice cream base, keep in mind that it will taste sweeter at room temperature than when it is frozen.

❖ Save your egg whites, because they will keep for up to 5 days in the refrigerator. You can use them in the Violet Coconut Macaroon recipe (see page 101), or in any of the meringue recipes (see pages 136–141).

❖ It is easy to flavor your ice cream base with vanilla beans or cinnamon sticks. Any of your favorite spices can make a delicious ice cream. Steep them like tea in the milk in step 3 (opposite), then strain. Here are a few guidelines:

❖ For Coffee Ice Cream: ¾ cup of freshly roasted whole coffee beans.

❖ For Vanilla Ice Cream: 1 vanilla bean, split, seeds scraped out.

❖ For Cinnamon Ice Cream: 1 short stick of soft Ceylon cinnamon.

❖ For Cardamom Ice Cream: 3 whole cardamom pods.

Raspberry Ripple Ice Cream

You can omit the vodka if you are making this for children, but it really lifts the flavor of the raspberries (and the spirits).

Makes: about 4½ cups
Preparation time: 30 minutes
Freezing time: up to 5 hours
WF GF V

1 quantity **Vanilla Ice Cream Base** (see above)
1⅔ cups **raspberries**
¼ cup **confectioners' sugar**
2 tablespoons **vodka**
2 teaspoons **vanilla extract**

1. Make the vanilla ice cream base.

2. Put the raspberries, confectioners' sugar, vodka and vanilla extract into a blender and process to a thick puree. Push through a strainer to remove the seeds.

3. Before the ice cream is completely frozen (but when it's pretty stiff), stir in the raspberries in thick seams. Continue to freeze in the freezer (see page 150) or in your ice cream machine.

Henry's Chocolate & Salted Caramel Ice Cream Bombe

An outrageous dessert to show off with. Don't worry about the calories—it is scientifically proven that anything you eat after dark doesn't make you fat.

Serves: 8
Preparation time: 45 minutes
Freezing time: 45 minutes (first churn)
+ 5 hours
WF GF V

For the ice cream
1¾ cups **heavy cream**
⅔ cup **milk**
4oz **chocolate** (70% cocoa solids)
5 **free-range egg yolks**
⅔ cup **superfine sugar**
⅓ cup **unsweetened cocoa powder**

For the caramel (crunchy nut toffee)
¾ cup **superfine sugar**
1¾ cups **heavy cream**
juice of ½ a **lemon**

For the cracknel
1 cup **sugar**
½ cup **hazelnuts**

My mom always used to make ice cream bombes when we were children. I remember one in particular that had a lemon ice cream exterior and grated dark chocolate inside, which tumbled out of it when you cut into it. I concocted this homage to those childhood bombes one Saturday, after I had promised to bring dessert to a friend's dinner party. It took me all day, and was gone in five minutes. You could say it went down a bomb.

HENRY

1. To make the ice cream, bring the cream and milk to a boil. Stir in the chocolate.

2. Put the egg yolks into a large bowl. Add the sugar and cocoa powder and beat well. Beat in a little of the hot cream-milk mixture, then put everything into a saucepan and return it to the stove. Heat gently, stirring well, for 10 minutes, and let simmer. Pour through a strainer and let cool.

3. Freeze in an ice cream machine according to the manufacturer's instructions. Or by hand (see page 150). Let the ice cream rest in the freezer, but not for too long. You need it softish to put the whole thing together.

4. To make the caramel, melt the sugar in a saucepan until it's a warm brown syrup. Slowly add the cream—it will whoosh up in an exciting fashion but will eventually settle down. Add a good pinch of sea salt. When all the sugar has dissolved in the cream, add the lemon juice. Let cool, then put into the refrigerator.

5. To make the cracknel, dissolve the sugar in a nonstick saucepan. Toss in the hazelnuts and pour onto an oiled sheet of wax paper. When it's cold, wrap the paper in a dish towel and give it a satisfying smash with a rolling pin.

6. To put it all together, line a deep baking dish with plastic wrap. Press three-quarters of the chocolate ice cream into the dish, leaving a well for the caramel. Scoop the cold caramel into the well. Seal the bombe with the remaining ice cream (this will be the base when you turn it out) Freeze for a good 5 hours or more.

7. Turn out onto a plate and sprinkle with the hazelnut cracknel.

❖ To serve, slice with a sharp knife dipped in hot water.

❖ This is not quite as hard to make as it sounds. The second one you make, however, is likely to be better than the first.

❖ Once you have got the hang of making bombes, you can have a lot of fun with them: lemon ice cream with grated chocolate; vanilla ice cream with a raspberry middle; chocolate ice cream with fresh mint ice cream inside. Have fun.

STEAMED PUDDINGS

Let's not kid ourselves: there is nothing healthy about a steamed pudding. It is, however, one of the greatest comfort foods ever invented. Hot, heavy, oozing sweetness, it can take the edge off the bitterest British winter. Ideally consumed after a long march through the frozen countryside, it may not do much for your arteries but it will certainly warm your soul.

Spotted Dick

A classic British pudding, with a classic British name.

Serves: 4–6
Preparation time: 20 minutes
Cooking time: 2½ hours

3 cups **all-purpose flour**
a pinch of **salt**
2 teaspoons **baking powder**
1 cup **vegetable suet** or **solid vegetable shortening**
½ cup firmly packed **brown sugar**
1¼ cups **dried currants**
grated zest of 1 **lemon**
½ teaspoon ground **allspice**
⅔ cup **whole milk**
butter, to grease and serve
light corn syrup, to serve

1. Sift the flour, salt, and baking powder into a large mixing bowl. Stir in the suet, sugar, currants, lemon zest, and allspice, then add just enough milk to make a soft dough.

2. Shape the dough into a log shape and wrap loosely in a sheet of buttered heavy-duty plastic wrap. Wrap this loosely in cheesecloth and secure with string.

3. Drop the log into a large saucepan of boiling water and simmer for 2 hours. If using a cylindrical mold, line it with buttered wax paper, put the dough in the mold and steam for 2½ hours.

4. To serve, remove the wrappings and cut the pudding into 1 inch slices. Serve with a pat of butter and drizzle with corn syrup.

TIPS

❖ You can substitute spelt flour for white flour if you prefer it.

❖ Serve with Quick Custard (see page 34) or heavy cream.

This dish was recently renamed "Spotted Richard" and then "Sultana Sponge" at a Welsh government cafeteria, after the catering staff complained of "immature comments" from council staff. The move was proclaimed ludicrous by one councilor, who campaigned successfully to have the proper name reinstated. People will soon be "frightened of their own shadow", he harrumphed. Makes you proud to be British.

HENRY

Jossy's Lemon Pudding Delicious

This pudding was one that Henry's great granny, Enid handed down to his mother. It was cut out from a newspaper and was called "Lemon Pudding"—next to it Enid had written "delicious!"

Serves: 6
Preparation time: 20 minutes
Cooking time: 40 minutes

V

4 tablespoons **unsalted butter**, at room temperature, plus extra for greasing
1 cup **superfine sugar**
finely grated zest and juice of 2 large **lemons**
4 exra-large **free-range eggs**, separated
⅓ cup **all-purpose flour**, plus ½ teaspoon **baking powder**
1 cup **whole milk**
½ teaspoon **cream of tartar**
confectioners' sugar, for sprinkling

1. Heat the oven to 350°F and place a roasting pan filled halfway with water on the center shelf to warm up. Butter a 1½–1¾ quart soufflé or other ovenproof dish.

2. Beat the butter in a large bowl until soft, then add the sugar and beat until fluffy. Gradually beat in the lemon juice, followed by the grated lemon zest and the egg yolks.

3. Sift the flour and baking powder onto the mixture and stir it in with a metal spoon, then gradually stir in the milk. Beat thoroughly until very smooth.

4. In a clean bowl, beat the egg whites with the cream of tartar using an electric handheld mixer until they stand in soft peaks. Then, using a metal spoon, fold them gently into the pudding mixture, about a quarter at a time.

5. Pour the mixture into the soufflé dish and stand it in the roasting pan of water in the oven. Bake for 40 minutes, or slightly less in a convection oven, until risen and golden brown on top.

6. Serve hot or cold, with a little confectioners' sugar sifted over the surface.

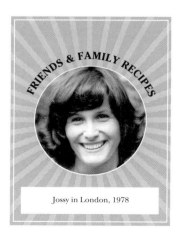

FRIENDS & FAMILY RECIPES

Jossy in London, 1978

St. Clement's Pudding

An old-fashion steamed pudding with a sticky, gooey top and the flavor of clementines infused throughout.

Serves: 4–6
Preparation time: 30 minutes
Cooking time: 2 hours

V

1 **clementine**

1 **vanilla bean**

1¼ sticks **unsalted butter**

⅔ cup **superfine sugar**

3 **eggs**, lightly beaten

1⅔ cups **all-purpose flour**

1½ teaspoons **baking powder**

½–⅔ cup **whole milk**

For the syrup
zest and juice of 2 **clementines**
1 cup **caster sugar**
⅔ cup **water**
heavy cream, to serve

1. Heat the oven to 325°F. Butter a medium, deep ovenproof dish.

2. Grate the zest from the clementine and scrape the seeds from the vanilla bean. Set the zested clementine and seeded vanilla bean aside for later.

3. Cream together the butter, sugar, clementine zest, and vanilla seeds until light and fluffy, then gradually add the beaten eggs.

4. Sift in the flour and baking powder and fold in thoroughly. Add the milk and set aside.

5. To make the syrup, put the clementine juice and zest into a small saucepan with the sugar, water and the vanilla bean. Heat gently, stirring until the sugar has dissolved, then bring to a boil and simmer until the mixture has reduced to a syrup.

6. Cut the zested clementine in half and place in the ovenproof dish with the cut sides down. Pour over three-quarters of the syrup, reserving the rest for later.

7. Spoon in the sponge mixture and place a circle of parchment paper on top, then cover the dish with a second larger piece of parchment paper (with a generous pleat in the middle) and secure with a rubber band or string.

8. Put the dish into a deep roasting pan and pour enough hot water into the pan to come halfway up the sides of the dish. Steam for about 2 hours, or until well risen and firm to the touch (remember to keep the water filled). Turn out onto a large serving dish deep enough to catch the syrup and pour the last of the syrup over the top. Serve with heavy cream.

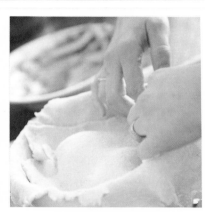

Sussex Pond Pudding

Suet, once a staple of the British pantry, has fallen out of fashion in recent years. However, it deserves its place in our culinary canon: nothing else can give a steamed pudding quite the same glossy, sticky crust. In this recipe, the juice from the orange mixes with the butter and sugar to create a devilish pool of syrup inside.

Serves: 6
Preparation time: 35 minutes
Cooking time: 2½ hours

For the dough

2 cups **all-purpose flour**, with 3 teaspoons **baking powder**
½ cup cold grated **suet** (or 1 stick **unsalted butter**)
⅔ cup **whole milk**

For the filling

½lb plus 5 tablespoons **unsalted butter**, softened
1 cup firmly packed **brown sugar**
⅓ cup **light corn syrup**
1 large unwaxed **orange**, pricked with a fork

1. In a bowl, gently toss together the flour and the suet or butter. Place in the freezer while you get the remaining ingredients together and prepare a deep 1½ quart ovenproof bowl by buttering it and dusting it with flour.

2. Remove the flour mixture from the freezer and add the milk, stirring with your hands to form a dough. Work quickly and do not overwork the dough. Wrap in plastic wrap and place in the refrigerator to rest.

3. To make the filling, beat the softened butter and brown sugar together well. Add the corn syrup and set aside.

4. Heat the oven to 325°F. Take the dough out of the refrigerator and lightly dust a work surface with flour. Roll the dough out to a circle that is large enough to fit your bowl. Use a paring knife to cut a wedge (about a quarter) out of the circle of dough. This will make the top of the pudding.

5. Put the circle of dough (with the wedge removed) into your prepared bowl and press the seams together where the wedge was removed to make a solid piece of dough. There should be about an inch of dough hanging over the rim of the bowl. Fill with the brown sugar mixture and place the pricked orange on top of that. Cover with the reserved wedge of dough. Take the excess dough that is hanging over the rim of the bowl and fold it over, sealing the lid. Cover with pleated parchment paper and tie with string or a rubber band.

6. Place the pudding in a deep roasting pan and pour enough hot water into the pan to come halfway up the sides of the bowl. Bake in the oven for 2–2½ hours, until golden. Remove from the oven and let sit for 5 minutes before carefully inverting onto a large serving dish deep enough to catch any syrup.

TIPS

You can replace the orange with the more traditional lemon if you prefer, or have both.

George's Ice Cream Sandwich

A dairy-free, sugar-free indulgent treat for you and any children in your life.

Makes: 12 circles
Preparation time: 10 minutes +
2 hours soaking
Cooking time: 2 hours
♥ ✓ WF GF DF V

1⅓ cups **almonds**
⅓ cup **shelled hemp seeds**
¾ cup **chopped fresh dates**
seeds of ½ a **vanilla bean**
a pinch of **sea salt**

I like these chewy cookies so much for their texture and lovely flavor. One of the wonderful benefits of eating sweets and cakes that are made with alternative ingredients is that they usually satisfy your cravings much better and you, therefore, eat less of them.

CLAIRE

1. Soak the almonds in water for 2 hours, drain, then crush to a paste in a mortar, or a food processor.

2. Heat the oven to 225°F.

3. Add the hemp seeds, chopped dates, vanilla seeds and salt to the almonds and bring everything together by pounding or processing for a few seconds.

4. Press out onto parchment paper and roll to ⅛ inch thickness. Use cutters to cut 2 inch circles. Re-roll any excess to get 12 circles. Dry out for 2 hours in a low oven.

5. To make the ice cream sandwich: take a scoop of Maggie's Coconut Kiss Ice Cream and sandwich it between 2 circles. Hand to small child. Be prepared to load washing machine (don't worry, it doesn't stain).

Maggie's Coconut Kiss Ice Cream

A rich, fruity, dairy-free, and "raw" ice cream.

Serves: 6–8
Preparation time: 20 minutes
Freezing time: overnight
♥ ✓ WF GF DF V

1¾ cups **coconut milk**
3 tablespoons **water**
1¾ cups **dried sour cherries**
¼ cup **palm sugar** or **brown sugar**
5 whole **cardamom pods**
zest of 2 **oranges**
a pinch of **sea salt**

Maggie worked as a raw chef and learned how to delicately balance the flavors inherent in some commonly used ingredients. The combination of coconut, cardamom, and a tangy berry here work so well. Maggie originally used dried black currants, but they can be difficult to track down, so I made it with sour cherries.

CLAIRE

1. Heat the coconut milk and water in a saucepan over low heat with the cherries, palm sugar and cardamom pods. Stir occasionally and crush the cherries with the back of the spoon until softened and a deep caramel color is achieved. Remove from the heat and let cool. Remove and discard the cardamom pods.

2. Add the orange zest and sea salt. Pass the mixture through a fine mesh strainer. Thoroughly chill, then pour into an ice cream machine and freeze, according to the manufacturer's instructions (or see page 150 for manual method).

COOKING WITH CHIL

DREN

All the neighborhood kids love Claire. She worries that this is only because she is always carrying an enormous tower of cake boxes. Certainly my three-year-old son, George, has an unfortunate habit of greeting her with the words: "Hello Claire. Can I have some cake?"

The truth is, he loves her because she is generous and funny—and she always has cake. Grown-ups don't come much better than that.

These are some of Claire's favorite recipes to cook with children.

HENRY

Cut-out Cookies

You need the right kind of dough to make cut-out cookies—one that holds its shape during cooking. This recipe should be a cornerstone of your baking repertoire, especially if you have young children. Make these crumbly, light cookies for Christmas, children's parties, or just because it's a great way to keep the kids entertained.

Makes: 24, depending on size
Preparation time: 15 minutes +
2 hours chilling time
Cooking time: 15 minutes
V

2 sticks **unsalted butter**, very soft
2 cups **superfine sugar**
2 **free-range eggs**
1 teaspoon **vanilla extract**
4½ cups **all-purpose flour**
1 teaspoon **baking powder**
a pinch of **salt**
Royal Icing (see page 179)

1. With an electric handheld mixer, beat the softened butter with the superfine sugar until light, pale and fluffy.

2. Add the eggs, one by one, then the vanilla extract.

3. Put the flour into a separate bowl and whisk in the baking powder and salt. Add half of this to the creamed mixture and beat on low speed until just combined.

4. Add the remaining flour mixture and beat again to combine well.

5. Divide the dough in half and wrap each ball in plastic wrap. You could freeze one ball for another time if you like. Chill for about 2 hours or overnight before using.

6. When ready to make the biscuits, heat the oven to 325°F. Line a couple of baking sheets with parchment paper.

7. Lightly dust a surface with flour, then roll out the dough to about ¼ inch thick. Cut out shapes with your cutters and transfer the cookies to your prepared baking sheets. Chill for 15–20 minutes, then bake for 15 minutes, or until just starting to turn golden. Transfer to a wire rack and let cool completely.

8. Decorate the cookies with royal icing and let stand overnight to dry.

9. Store in an airtight container for up to a week.

TIPS

❖ Try adding flavors to the cookies for variation. Anita (who designed this book) put a ½ teaspoon of ground apple pie spice into her Halloween Cookies (see page 253), which made them deliciously autumnal. You could also add lemon zest, cinnamon, or other spices you like. Henry is quite fond of ground cardamom seeds for a scented flavor.

❖ If you're making these with children, you really should to let them do the decorating. Lay out a lot of little bowls filled with sugary things to stick on to the icing—sprinkles, silver sugar balls, M&Ms, whatever—and let them go mental.

PURÉES

ICINGS

Greengage

Quince

Rhubarb

Raspberry

Strawberry

Turmeric

Royal Icing

Swooped over a fruitcake or drizzled on cut-out cookies, royal icing is an old-fashion edible decoration that—although incredibly sugary—is as classy as the name suggests.

You don't need to reach for artificial colorings (although sometimes we think it's OK and sort of fun). Puree brightly colored fruit to make natural colorings instead (see tips below), or try using powdered turmeric for a gorgeous yellow icing with a delicate aniseedy flavor.

Makes: about 1¾lb,
or enough to cover an 8–9 inch cake
Preparation time: 10 minutes
Cooking time: none
♥ WF GF DF V

4 **free-range egg whites**
5½ cups **confectioners' sugar**
½ cup **water** or **fruit puree**

1. Put all the ingredients together in a bowl and use an electric handheld mixer on low speed to mix until combined. Then turn the speed up to medium for about 7 minutes, or until thick ribbons form.

2. You can make the icing softer or looser by adding a little more water.

TIPS

✤ Puree fruits that are fresh, ripe, and vibrant-colored by simply blending them to a pulp in a blender. Strain the puree to remove seeds and skin (except in the case of strawberries, which seem to benefit from keeping their little seeds in).

S'mores

This is not a recipe as much as a part of growing up. Children learn to make s'mores —so named because everyone wants some more—from a very early age. They symbolize summer camp, ghost stories, and, in a way, independence. Toast the marshmallows as much or as little as you like. We've used plain cookies, but feel free to use Graham crackers to make the classic s'mores.

Makes: enough for 6
Preparation time: 5 minutes
Cooking time: 2 minutes

V

2 bags of **marshmallows**
6 bars of your favorite **chocolate**
2 packets of **plain cookies** or **Graham crackers**
long skewers, for roasting

1. Build a campfire, or have an adult build one.

2. Bring all the ingredients out to the campfire.

3. Gather your own personal supply of marshmallows and cookies, and your chocolate bar.

4. Take 1 cookie and top it with a piece of chocolate. Set aside.

5. Get cozy.

6. Push 2 or 3 marshmallows onto a skewer while listening to ghost stories. Hold the end of the stick just above the flame to char the marshmallows. We like them golden but just starting to burn.

7. When you have charred them to your liking, quickly press the marshmallow onto the chocolate and sandwich with another cookie.

8. Devour.

 TIPS

✤ Sometimes the marshmallows will go up in flames. This is OK, just blow out the flame.

GUARANTEED
SATISFACTION

A Good Chocolate Cake

A great cake for a children's party if you don't want your house terrorized by children high on sugar and food coloring. It is vegan, but they'll never know it. It also looks ravishing decorated with flowers from your yard.

Serves: 8
Preparation time: 30 minutes
Cooking time: 35 minutes
Cooling and decorating time: 2 hours
♥ ✓ DF V

For the cake
⅔ cup hot **water**
1 cup **unsweetened cocoa powder**
scant 1 cup **agave syrup**
scant 1 cup **coconut milk**
juice of ½ a **lemon**
⅓ cup **sunflower oil**
2 teaspoons **vanilla extract**
1⅔ cups **spelt flour** or 1½ cups **all-purpose flour**
½ teaspoon **baking powder**
1½ teaspoons **baking soda**
a pinch of **salt**

For the icing
¼ cup **coconut oil**
8oz **dark chocolate**
1 teaspoon **vanilla extract**
3 tablespoons **agave syrup**

flowers from your yard, to decorate (optional)

1. Heat the oven to 325°F. Grease and line an 8–9 inch cake pan with parchment paper.

2. Beat together the hot water and cocoa powder until smooth. Add the remaining wet ingredients and set aside.

3. In a large bowl, sift together the flour, baking powder, baking soda and salt. Pour the wet mixture over the dry and beat in a circular motion from the center of the bowl, moving outwards to combine. Pour the mixture into the cake pan.

4. Bake in the oven for about 35 minutes, or until a toothpick inserted comes out clean and the cake is springy to the touch. Let the cake cool for 10 minutes before turning it out onto a wire rack to cool completely.

5. For the frosting, put all the ingredients into a heatproof bowl, place over a saucepan of barely simmering water to melt, and stir. Move the cake to a serving plate and drizzle the frosting over it. If you like, decorate with flowers from your yard.

TIPS

Instead of flowers, you could add some raspberries to the cake and arrange a few on top for decoration.

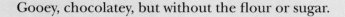

Maggie's Best Chocolate Chip Cookies

Gooey, chocolatey, but without the flour or sugar.

Makes: 24
Preparation time: 15 minutes
Cooking time: 11 minutes
WF GF V

2¼ cups **gluten-free flour**
2 teaspoons **baking soda**
½ teaspoon **sea salt**
1 cup **semisweet chocolate chips** or chunks
3 tablespoons **agave nectar**
1 cup **maple syrup**
1 stick **unsalted butter**, melted
1 tablespoon **vanilla extract**
sea salt, for sprinkling (optional)

1. Heat the oven to 350°F. Line a baking sheet with parchment paper.

2. Mix together all the dry ingredients in a medium bowl (including the chocolate chips or chunks).

3. Mix together all the wet ingredients in a small bowl.

4. Add the wet ingredients to the dry ingredients, and stir until they are well combined, but do not overmix.

5. Drop spoonfuls of the cookie dough onto the prepared baking sheet. Lightly sprinkle with sea salt, if desired.

6. Bake in the oven for only 11 minutes, and let the cookies cool on the sheet for 1 minute before transferring to a cooling rack.

TIPS

❖ These are even better the next day. Enjoy with a glass of cold Hazelnut Milk (see page 56).

❖ Following the baking time instructions will give you the perfect gooey texture.

❖ If you can't get hold of gluten-free flour and you don't mind the gluten, normal flour can be substituted.

Once you have got the hang of these, you can play around with the recipe. We like to substitute white chocolate and dried blueberries for the dark chocolate, and add milk chocolate and toasted pecans, or walnuts or hazelnuts in with the dark chocolate in the original recipe. Maggie is one of the bakers we love (see page 232). In her original recipe, she uses all-purpose flour, not gluten-free, and maple sugar instead of agave syrup. I substituted agave syrup here because maple sugar is difficult to find in the UK. She also sometimes adds ½ teaspoon of molasses, which sounds divine.

CLAIRE

Technicolor Dreamcake

A really fun cake to make, and lurid enough—despite the natural colors—to satisfy any child. The idea came from an old cake book Claire picked up at a thrift shop.

Serves: 10–12
Preparation time: 25 minutes
Cooking time: 50 minutes
V

For the cake

2⅓ cups **all-purpose flour**

½ teaspoon **salt**

4 teaspoons **baking powder**

1¾ sticks **unsalted butter**, very soft

2 cups **sugar**

1 teaspoon **vanilla extract**

4 **free-range eggs**, separated

1 cup **milk**

For EACH of the three layers of frosting:

1 tablespoon **fresh fruit purée** for each layer, strained (we used raspberry, quince, turmeric, and strawberry)

2 tablespoons **unsalted butter**, softened

1¼ cups **confectioners' sugar**

lemon juice or **vanilla extract**

1. Heat the oven to 325°F. Grease 2 x 9 inch cake pans and line them with parchment paper.

2. In a large bowl, sift together the flour, salt, and baking powder and set aside.

3. Cream the butter and sugar until fluffy. Add the vanilla, then the egg yolks, one at a time, mixing well after each addition. Add half the milk and mix well. Add half the flour mixture and combine. Repeat with the remaining milk and flour.

4. Beat the egg whites in a separate bowl until soft peaks form. Stir a third of the egg whites into the cake mixture to lighten the batter and then fold in the remainder, being careful not to knock out too much air in the process.

5. Carefully spoon the mixture equally into the pans and bake in the oven for 45–50 minutes, or until a toothpick inserted comes out clean. Let the cakes cool for 10 minutes before taking them out of the pans and letting them cool completely on a wire rack.

6. Slice each layer in two and place the bottom of one on a cake stand. Slather with your favorite frosting flavors (see page 178 for inspiraton), then continue to stack up the layers. The top layer looks great with a buttercream or Royal Icing (see page 179) that drizzles down the sides. Top with fresh fruit.

    To make the frosting, strain the fruit puree and set aside. In a medium bowl, beat the butter and sugar until light and fluffy. Add the fruit purée, then taste. A little lemon juice or vanilla can balance the flavors of your frosting nicely.

SPELT LOAF • STARTERS • GLUTEN-FREE BREAD
RYE BREAD • CRUSTY WHITE ROLLS • SODA BREAD

BREAD
& SAVORIES

FLATBREAD • PIZZA • OATMEAL COOKIES

WITHOUT BREAD, WE WOULD HAVE NO CIVILIZATION.

Civilization requires surplus. When man worked out how to exploit wild grains—to store them during the winter months and multiply them again during the summer—he no longer needed to spend his life roaming about in search of food. He finally had a modicum of time on his hands, which he spent learning new skills, such as writing, architecture, making music, and generally starting down the long road toward culture. Thanks to bread, we have *American Idol* and line dancing.

The early breads—first made about 12,000 years ago in the Fertile Crescent of the Middle East—were solid cakes made from ground pastes of barley and the earliest strains of wheat, einkorn, and emmer. These dense patties still have their descendants around the globe—in Indian chapatis, Mexican tortillas, and crumbly Scottish oatmeal cookies (see recipe on page 212).

Bread making was transformed when yeast was first introduced to raise the dough and make lighter, softer loaves. Yeasted breads are first mentioned in the literature of the Egyptians, but the chances are that this breakthrough was made much earlier, as any mixture of wheat and water, left out, will turn spontaneously into bubbling sourdough, powered by the natural yeasts that live on the grains. You can repeat this experiment—as wondrous as any in gastronomy—by following the recipe on page 195–7.

Unfortunately, over the last century many of the supposed advances in bread making have, in fact, stripped the goodness from this elemental food. Ancient strains of wheat have been selectively bred to increase yields and gluten content. This has had two unwelcome side effects: Modern wheat contains fewer nutrients and far more of the proteins that trigger inflammatory reactions. Hence, the massive increase in wheat intolerance and allergy. Most bread is also now made using the Chorleywood process, which was introduced in the 1960s and uses hardened vegetable fat, intense energy, very high volumes of yeast, and many additives to reduce the time required to make bread (and, therefore, its cost). A traditional loaf of bread contains four ingredients: water, salt, wheat, and yeast. A typical Chorleywood loaf contains more than 20 ingredients.*

The bread recipes in this book all use traditional methods. We favor ancient grains such as spelt and rye, and there's even an entirely gluten-free loaf. None of which, incidentally, means that these loaves are remotely academic or complicated to make. Homemade bread is in fact one of the easiest ways to put the goodness—and the pleasure—back into your daily diet.

*For further reading on this, see Andrew Whitley's excellent book *Bread Matters*.

Bread—The Basics

TYPES OF BREAD

All breads fall into four main categories, defined by what makes them rise:

SOURDOUGH

Sourdough is the most ancient form of leavened bread. It is made with a sourdough starter (see page 195), which can either be taken from someone else's existing starter or created by leaving wheat and water to ferment naturally. The starter contains a symbiotic combination of natural yeasts and lactobacillus culture. It is the culture that creates the lactic acid that gives this bread its distinctive sour taste.

Sourdough has a reputation for being frustrating and unpredictable if you don't make it all the time, because the starter needs attention. But starters are surprisingly robust—Henry, being chaotic and absent-minded, has had to bring many a forgotten and slimy starter back to life.

The thing that takes some getting used to is the timing—the cycle for making a loaf is a minimum of twelve hours, and typically twenty-four. However, the actual work involved is minimal (most of that time is spent waiting for the dough to rise), and the reward is a uniquely flavored loaf that stays fresh for over a week.

YEASTED BREADS

Most bread is risen using baker's yeast, the species *Saccharomyces Cerevisiae*. It is the same yeast that is used to brew alcohol. It feeds on the sugars in the wheat and converts them into carbon dioxide, the gas that causes the bread to rise. It is easier to use than a sourdough because it does not require looking after and it is a good deal more vigorous—a loaf can rise in a couple of hours in a warm room. You can buy yeast fresh in blocks or dried in granules.

If you have not made bread before, this is the way to start. The simple spelt loaf on page 193 is outrageously easy to make and equally impressive. You can also experiment with different flour mixtures and flavorings to create your own signature loaf.

If you have some sourdough in the refrigerator, you can add a little to traditionally yeasted breads to get a touch of the flavor in under half the time.

SODA BREAD

This bread uses baking soda as its leavening agent. Wheat flour is mixed with buttermilk (or sometimes yogurt) and the lactic acid reacts with the baking soda to create bubbles of carbon dioxide, which raise the bread.

It is a relatively modern bread, having become popular in Ireland in the mid-nineteenth century as a cheaper and faster alternative to yeast. It has a wonderful soft, cakey texture and a distinctive taste.

UNLEAVENED BREAD

This is a dough that requires no leavening agent at all. It is the easiest of all breads to make.

A few RULES of thumb

Whichever of the above breads you are attempting, there are a few rules worth remembering:

BREAD BAKING IS NOT AN EXACT SCIENCE

The specific batch of flour you are using, the quality of the yeast and water, atmospheric temperature and humidity, and the foibles of your oven will all affect how your loaf turns out.

BE PREPARED TO FOLLOW YOUR INSTINCTS

That might mean leaving it to rise a little longer on a cold day, adding some more water if the dough feels dry.

IT CAN'T GO THAT WRONG

Don't worry about creating the perfect loaf. You will learn more from experimenting than from doing it the same way every time. Even the ugliest-looking efforts generally taste good.

WETTER IS BETTER

If you are wondering whether your bread is too wet, don't automatically add more flour. It is almost always better wetter.

ADD STEAM FOR THE PERFECT CRUST

Putting a cup of water in a baking sheet at the bottom of the oven works wonders to create a glossy crust.

WRITE IT DOWN

There are few things more maddening than creating a great loaf and not being able to remember quite how you tweaked the recipe. Take notes.

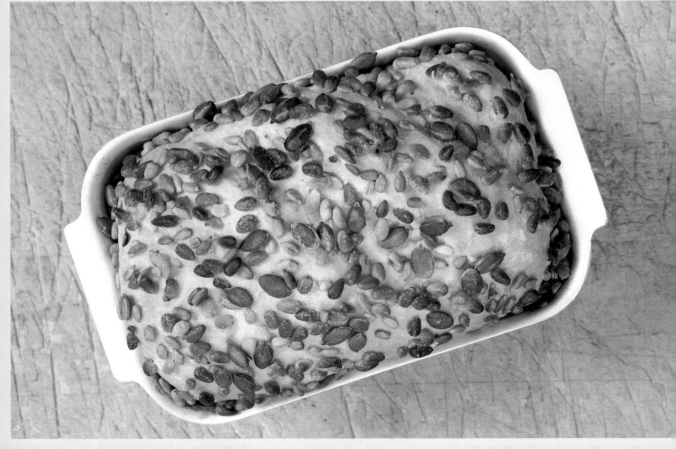

Spelt Bread & variations

This is a bread that Henry has been baking for years, at his wife's insistence.
It is very easy to make and impossible to get wrong. It is also a great recipe to
play with—adding nuts and seeds, mixing in spices, and using different flours.

Makes: 3 loaves
Preparation time: 10 minutes
+ 2 hours rising time
Cooking time: 40 minutes
♥ ✓ V
(DF if you use oil for greasing)

soft **butter**, for greasing
1.5kg **strong wholemeal spelt flour**
2 x 14oz envelopes **dry active yeast**
2 tablespoons **sea salt**, crushed
1 cup **pine nuts**
⅔ cup **pumpkin seeds**
scant 1 cup **sunflower seeds**
½ cup **extra virgin olive oil**
3¾–4¼ cups warm **water**
⅓ cup **sunflower seeds** and **nuts**,
    to sprinkle on top

When Henry's wife gave birth
to each of their sons, he baked
her a version of this bread full
of the spices that are said to
encourage lactation. It seems
to work. To make bread that
will fill your breasts with milk,
add 1 tablespoon each of anise
seeds, caraway seeds, fennel
seeds and fenugreek (ground
in a mortar and pestle or coffee
grinder). This has no impact
on men or woman who aren't
breast-feeding, and we think it
is the most delicious of all.

1. Grease 3 x 9 inch loaf pans with butter.

2. Mix all the dry ingredients (except the seeds for the top)
   together in a bowl large enough to knead the dough in.

3. Add the oil, then the water, stirring until the mixture sticks together. Knead in the
   bowl for a few minutes, until smooth. You can add a little flour if it is too sticky, but
   remember the maxim—wetter is better. It doesn't matter if a little sticks to your hands.

4. Cut into 3 pieces, shape into vague ovals, then put into the loaf pans. Cut a
   pattern in deep gashes on the top and sprinkle the reserved seeds into the
   gashes, sprinkling a little spelt flour (or bran if you have some on hand) all over.

5. Put the pans into a large plastic trash bag and tuck the ends of the bag under
   the tins, leaving them enclosed with plenty of air. Let rest until the dough has
   doubled in size. This will take about 2 hours in a warm kitchen.

6. Bake at 450°F for 20 minutes, then turn the temperature down to 400°F for
   another 20 minutes. Turn out and cool on a rack.

TIPS

❖ These freeze really well in freezer bags, but don't keep bread in the refrigerator
  because it turns stale more quickly.

❖ You can use normal whole-wheat flour if you can't get spelt. Or if you like your loaf
  lighter, you can replace 4½ cups of the spelt flour with 3⅔ cups white bread flour.

❖ Experiment with all kinds of additions. Breads with nuts and fruit in can be
  amazing. Try date and almond, or apricot and walnut.

❖ Play with herbs and spices: rosemary, dill, and oregano are all interesting.

SOURDOUGH STARTER

If you can't find a kindly soul to give you some starter, here are tips on how to make one—courtesy of master baker Tom Herbert, of Hobbs House Bakery in Gloucestershire, who gave Henry a piece of the starter that has been handed down in his family for 55 years.

STARTING A SOURDOUGH

Find a suitable container to house your sourdough—a preserving jar is ideal. Clean it well and weigh it while empty, noting the weight on an address tag or label (this will save you having to empty it out to know how much you have left in the future).

Put equal amounts of flour and warm water into your jar, such as 1 cup of flour and 1 cup of warm water, and stir. Organic whole-wheat flour, dark rye flour, and whole-grain spelt flour all work really well. Put the jar in a prominent and warm place in your kitchen (this will be its second home), with the lid sealed.

Each day for a week repeat the feeding process. Put ½ cup of the starter in a bowl (you can use the surplus to flavor cakes, rolls, pancakes, and pizza dough), add 1 cup of water and 1 cup of flour and stir vigorously with a clean finger or a fork to remove all floury lumps. Return it to the jar.

After about 5 days you'll notice bubbles in the dough—like the first windy smile of a baby. You can start to use it after a week, but it'll be slow, weak, and infantile. From now on, you can keep it in the refrigerator (its first home), removing it a couple of days before use to feed it back into full bubbly liveliness (using ½ cup of starter, 1 cup of flour and 1 cup of water as before). After a month, the dough will have matured and you'll get a better, more even flavor and rising performance.

If it is not performing well enough, try taking it out of the refrigerator and giving it an extra feed. Remember that it is a living culture—if it's not hibernating in the refrigerator where it can survive for several months—and it likes to be fed, warm, and aerated (stirred). If it dies, you'll know because it'll smell like a dead dog on a hot day. Trash the lot and start again.

I'm the custodian of our family sourdough, which has been raising award-winning loaves at Hobbs House Bakery for over fifty-five years. Who will you leave your sourdough to in your will?

Peace and loaf,
Tom Herbert

Opposite: Whole-grain spelt starter (above), white wheat starter (below).

TOM (RIGHT) AND BROTHER GEORGE, MONTE CARLO, 1981

Sourdough bread

There are two stages to making a sourdough: the "sponge"—a reinvigorated starter—and the "dough".

Makes: 1 loaf
Preparation time: 14 hours
(including rising)
Cooking time: 35–40 minutes
♥ DF V

For the sponge
¾ cup **water** at about 80°F
½ cup **sourdough starter** (see page 195) brought to room temperature
2½ cups **white bread flour** (organic here makes a big difference; the chemicals used to kill pests on the growing wheat will also kill the good organisms needed for the bread to rise properly when using a natural yeast)
½ teaspoon **fine sea salt**

For the dough:
6 tablespoons **water** at 80°F
3 cups **strong white bread flour**
1 tablespoon **fine sea salt**

1. **The sponge:** In a medium bowl or container that will fit into your refrigerator, combine the water, starter, and white bread flour with a wooden spoon.

2. It is fine if there are lumps of flour or starter because as the sponge starts working it will all meld together. It will have a wonderfully soft and bouncy consistency—too wet to form a dough at this stage.

3. Set this aside in a warm area of your kitchen, draped with a clean cloth or plastic wrap. Ideally, the temperature should be in the lower 80's°F. This is easy on a hot summer's day, but in the winter or spring, you might put it near the radiator or the oven while doing other cooking. Let this rise for 4 hours.

4. **The dough:** Put the sponge into a mixing bowl. You can mix by hand, of course, but if you have a freestanding mixer with a dough hook, it will make the job easier. Add all of the dough ingredients and mix for about 8–10 minutes. You should end up with a smooth and elastic dough that is just slightly tacky.

5. If you must knead by hand to feel like you are really making bread, then now is your chance (see page 40). You really don't need to put flour down on your work surface, so avoid this temptation. Put the dough back in the bowl and cover it again and place it back in its warm spot for 3–4 hours.

6. Line a bowl with cheese cloth or a clean dish towel and generously dust it with flour. Turn the dough out on to your work surface and bash it around to punch some of the air out. This also gets the yeasts acting again. Then shape it into a round loaf shape. Put the dough into the flour-lined bowl and cover it with another cloth. Let it sit in the warm spot for about 5 hours.

7. This is very important: Turn your oven on a good 45 minutes before you are ready to put the dough inside it. Get it good and hot, as hot as your oven will go. Claire uses an oven thermometer to check that it is at its maximum before proceeding.

8. Put a baking sheet into the oven and get it really hot, and place a baking pan (to hold a shallow depth of water) on the floor of your oven. Prepare a large measuring cup of water next to the oven, ready to pour into the pan. Now, uncover your loaf.

9. When everything is ready, remove the hot baking sheet from the oven and quickly close the door. It is so important to keep the heat in there. Now, turn the dough out onto the baking sheet and slice four slits into the top in the shape of a square (or you can develop your own signature cut).

10. Quickly open the oven, slide the baking sheet in, and pour a few glugs of water into the pan on the floor of your oven (be careful the steam does not burn your hand) and slam the door fast.

11. Set your timer for 20 minutes, and don't peek. Then take a look and you may find it will need another 15–20 minutes. Claire likes her loaf to get nice and dark, even burned in places. Cool on a wire rack.

Gluten-Free Bread

The gluten in a loaf gives it that chewy interior and tender crumb. Take the gluten out and you get something a little denser of crumb and a bit more cakelike. In its own right, however, it is very satisfying.

Makes: 1 loaf
Preparation time: 20 minutes
+ 1 hour rising time
Cooking time: 55 minutes
♥ WF GF V

4 cups **gluten-free whole-wheat bread flour**
½ teaspoon **sea salt**
2 x (14oz) envelopes **dry active yeast**
2 tablespoons **honey**
1⅓ cups **milk**
1 tablespoon **cider vinegar**
2 tablespoons **olive oil**
2 **free-range eggs**
poppy seeds, to sprinkle

1. Grease an 8 inch loaf pan.

2. Combine the flour, salt and yeast and set aside.

3. Warm the honey and milk slightly and remove from the heat. Add the vinegar and oil and beat in the eggs.

4. Add the wet ingredients to the dry ingredients and bring together to form a dough. Then shape the dough into a log. Place it in your prepared pan, sprinkle with water, and then scatter poppy seeds over the top to cover. Put the dough in a warm place and let rise for 1 hour.

5. Heat the oven to 400°F and bake for 45–55 minutes.

6. Let cool in the pan for 5 minutes before turning out onto a wire rack to cool completely.

TIPS

✤ Try adding some seeds to the dough to vary the texture and flavor of this loaf. It is always a good idea to soak the seeds overnight before adding them to the bread mixture, because soaking the seeds increases the amount of vitamins your body can absorb from them.

Flour Station Rye Bread

We use this bread at Leon to make the New York-style open sandwiches we serve for breakfast. It is baked for us by the magnificent bakers at London's Flour Station, who add baked potato to the dough to keep it moist. It has a wonderful springy texture, with nutty sunflower seeds adding bite.

Makes: 1 loaf
Preparation time: 1 hour
+ resting and rising time
Cooking time: 55 minutes
♥ ✓ WF DF V

2 tablespoons **rye starter** (50% water/50% rye flour)
1 medium **baking potato**
1½ teaspoons **water**
1 cup **rye flour**, plus extra for dusting
½oz **dried yeast**
2 teaspoons **salt**
1 cup **sunflower seeds**
2 tablespoons **molasses**

1. First make your rye starter as you would a wheat or spelt starter (see page 195).

2. Bake the potato and let cool, then peel.

3. Put all the ingredients into a mixing bowl (avoiding direct contact between the yeast and the salt).

4. In a freestanding mixer with a dough hook, mix on slow speed until everything is blended, or mix by hand. The dough will be very wet and sticky, but after a while the color will change slightly from brown to a lighter, more yellow color.

5. Cover the bowl with a damp cloth and let the dough rest for approximately 3 hours, or until the dough is "active" or bubbling.

6. Butter a 9 inch loaf psn and dust it with rye flour.

7. Dust the table with rye flour and turn out the dough. Shape and place in the prepared loaf pan. Press down lightly and dust the top with rye flour.

8. Leave in a warm, draft-free place to "prove" (or rise), until you see cracks appearing on the surface of the dough. It should increase in size by approximately 50 percent.

9. Heat the oven to 425°F. Dust the dough with rye flour again and bake in the oven for 55 minutes, or until the loaf has a rich dark crust.

TIPS

❖ This bread actually improves with age and is best enjoyed the day after baking. It will stay fresh for at least a week, because the potato attracts moisture and, therefore, keep the bread moist for longer.

❖ Toast thin slices of this bread and top with butter or coconut oil and a Nut Butter (see page 57).

Raab the Bakers
Crusty White Rolls

Sometimes there's nothing to compare with some crusty white bread—despite its shortcomings in the nutrition department. Mima and Henry recently spit-roasted a lamb for a birthday party in their yard (the lamb took up about a third of the yard). We served it with mint sauce, and Claire suggested crispy white rolls from this family baker in Islington, London. They really hit the spot.

Makes: 10–12
Preparation time: 30 minutes +
1½ hours resting time
Cooking time: 20 minutes
♥ V

1 x (0.6oz) **fresh yeast cake**
⅔–1 cup **warm water**
½ cup warm **milk**
a pinch of **sugar**
2 cups **white bread flour**
1 teaspoon **salt**
¼ cup **white vegetable shortening** or **vegetable oil**
ice cubes

1. Put the water into a bowl, add the yeast, and stir to dissolve. Add the milk and a pinch of sugar to help activate the yeast.

2. Place the flour, salt, and shortening on a work surface, making a well in the middle (if using vegetable oil, add it in the next step).

3. Pour the liquid yeast mixture into the well and gradually blend it into the flour to form a dough, mixing it all together with your hands. Add a little more flour to prevent sticking and knead for 10–12 minutes, until a smooth elastic dough is achieved.

4. Place the dough in an oiled bowl, cover it with a damp dish towel, and let it rest in a warm place for an hour, or until it has doubled in size.

5. Tip the dough onto a floured work surface and divide it into 10–12 pieces. Shape them into circles, pressing down with your hands using a circular motion.

6. Place the rolls on a baking sheet lined with silicone paper or oiled well, leaving enough room for the rolls not to touch once they have risen. Cut a slit in the top of each roll with a sharp knife. Cover with a dish towel.

7. Preheat the oven to 425°F and place an empty baking sheet at the bottom of the oven.

8. When the rolls have doubled in size, place the sheet in the oven. At the same time as the rolls go in, throw approximately 10 ice cubes onto the hot empty baking sheet at the bottom of the oven and shut the oven door. This will create steam, which is essential for a crusty roll. Bake for 15–20 minutes, or until golden brown.

NO CHILDREN WERE HARMED IN THE TAKING OF THESE PHOTOGRAPHS

Ballymaloe Brown Soda Bread

A classic version of this yeast-free, cakey, breakfast bread.

Makes: 1 large loaf or 2 small loaves
Preparation time: 10 minutes
Cooking time: 40 minutes

♥ ✓ V

2⅓ cups **brown whole-wheat flour** (preferably **stone-ground**)
2⅓ cups **all-purpose flour**
2 teaspoons **sea salt**
2 teaspoons **baking soda**, sifted
2⅓ cups **buttermilk** or **sour milk**

1. Heat the oven to 450°F.

2. Mix all the dry ingredients together in a large wide bowl, then make a well in the center and pour in all the buttermilk or sour milk.

3. Using one hand, stir in a full circle, starting in the center and working toward the outside of the bowl until all the flour is incorporated. The dough should be soft but not too wet and sticky. When it all comes together, in a matter of seconds, turn it out onto a well-floured board.

4. WASH AND DRY YOUR HANDS.

5. Roll the dough around gently with floury hands for a second, just enough to tidy it up. Flip it over and flatten slightly, to about 2 inches.

6. Sprinkle a little flour onto a baking sheet and place the loaf on top of the flour.

7. Make a deep cross with a knife on top of the loaf and bake in the oven for 15–20 minutes. Reduce the heat to 400°F and bake for approximately another 15–20 minutes, or until the bread is cooked (in some ovens it may be necessary to turn the bread upside down on the baking sheet for 5–10 minutes before the end of baking).

8. When the bread is ready, it will sound hollow when tapped. Cool on a wire rack.

TIPS

❖ You can add 2 tablespoons of oats, 1 egg, and 1 tablespoon of butter to the above to make a richer soda bread dough.

This recipe is from *Ballymaloe Cookery Course* by Darina Allen (Kyle Cathie, 2001)

Darina Allen and her family have been running the Ballymaloe Cookery School in East Cork, Ireland, for nearly thirty years. The school is set within ten acres of market gardens, greenhouses, and orchards—themselves set in hundreds of acres of organic farmland. Stepping through the little wooden gate into the courtyard of the school is like entering another world. I have been lucky enough to have been invited over there a number of times to give cooking demos, and the thing I most look forward to is the breakfast, especially when the previous day's lesson included making soda bread.

CLAIRE

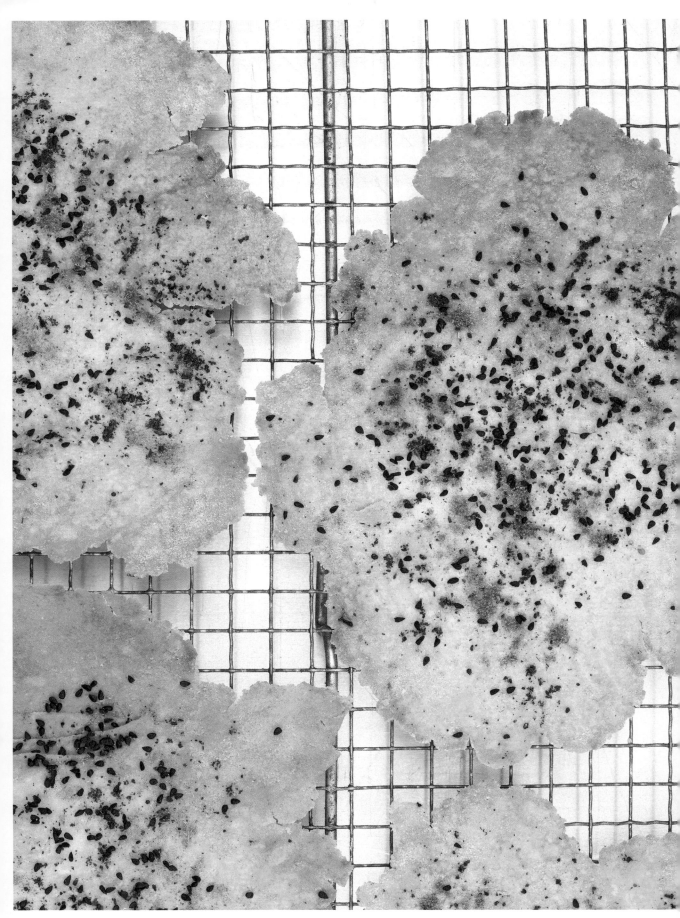

Flatbread with Zatar

This flatbread actually contains a small amount of yeast, which gives it a little lift. The texture of the dough is very dry while you are making it and feels similar to a pasta dough. Look for semolina and Italian "00" flour in Italian delicatessns or on the Internet. They are worth seeking out for their unique texture.

Makes: 10
Preparation time: 2 hours
Cooking time: 10 minutes
♥ DF V

1 x (¼oz) envelope active **dry yeast**
scant ½ cup warm **water**
3 tablespoons **olive oil**
1⅔ cups **fine semolina** or 2½ cups **spelt flour**
½ cup **"00" flour** or **all-purpose flour**
1 teaspoon **sea salt**
10 teaspoons **zatar**

1. Dissolve the yeast in the warm water in the bottom of a large mixing bowl. Pour in the olive oil, add the semolina, flour, and salt, and coarsely mix it all together with your hands or a wooden spoon to make a dough.

2. Cover the bowl and set the dough in a warm place to rise for about 1½ hours.

3. When the dough has rested, divide it into 10 pieces and roll each piece into a ball. Let the dough rest again for 10 minutes.

4. Heat the oven to 450°F.

5. Flatten each ball of dough with your hands and cover with a damp towel for about 30 minutes.

6. Sprinkle the flatbreads with zatar and place on baking sheets in the oven for about 10 minutes, until crisp and golden. Cool on a wire rack.

TIPS

❖ Zatar is a flavoring that can be found in Middle Eastern stores. If you can't find it, you can make your own by mixing together ground spices—typically thyme, sesame seeds, and sumac. Cumin, coriander, and nigella seeds also work well.

❖ You could also make it without zatar—sprinkle with a little flaky sea salt once cooked and serve with really good green olive oil.

French Onion Tart

This recipe is an adaptation of the French classic *pissaladiere*, but made with spelt flour. It is very simple and very versatile. The possibilities for alternative toppings are endless.

Serves: 8 as a canapé or 4 for lunch
Preparation time: 30 minutes
Cooking time: 30 minutes
♥ V

Spelt pastry dough:
1 cup, 2 tablespoons **spelt flour**
pinch of **salt**
pinch of **sugar**
7 tablespoons cold **unsalted butter**, cut into pieces
¼ cup **iced water**

Topping:
3 tablespoons **olive oil**
2 **onions**, thinly sliced
1 teaspoon **vinegar**
½ cup **black olives**
6 **anchovies**
small bunch of **thyme**
1 **free-range egg**, beaten
salt and **black pepper**

To make the spelt pastry dough:

1. Combine the spelt flour, salt, and sugar in a bowl and cut in the butter with a knife. Leave larger chunks of butter than you would think (about the size of a garlic clove) to make the pastry more flaky.

2. Drizzle in the water and bring it all together in a ball.

3. Wrap in plastic wrap, and let it rest in the refrigerator for at least 30 minutes.

Meanwhile, make the topping:

4. Heat the oil in a heavy-based saucepan and add the sliced onions. Stir occasionally to be sure they don't burn. You are looking for a caramelized but soft onion.

5. Once cooked (in about 7–8 minutes) add the vinegar and 2 teaspoons of water. Sprinkle with thyme leaves and transfer into a bowl to cool.

6. Heat oven to 325°F.

7. Pit and break up the olives a little. On a floured surface, roll out the dough to approximately ⅛ inch thick and transfer to a baking sheet. Arrange the cooled onions, anchovies, and olives over the dough, leaving a small boarder, and season with salt and pepper.

8. Brush the edges with beaten egg, then bake in the oven for 25–30 minutes.

TIPS

✦ These are some of our favorite alternative toppings:

- **BUFFALO** Onions, slices of buffalo mozzarella, and tomato. Basil. Drizzle of olive oil.

- **SAUSAGE & SAGE** Onions and pieces of sausage and chopped sage.

- **TOMATO & THYME** Fine layer of Dijon mustard. Onions and slices of tomato. Thyme.

- **BROCCOLI & GOATS CHEESE** Onions. Finely chopped pieces of broccoli. Crumble on goats cheese after cooking.

Pizza Dough

This is a softer, thicker version of pizza dough than the thin-crust pizzas that are everywhere at the moment. It is supereasy to make and supercomforting to eat.

Makes: 2 pizzas
Preparation time: 4 hours
Cooking time: 30 minutes
♥ DF V

1 teaspoon **dried yeast**
1½–2 cups **water**
4 cups **"00" flour**
olive oil

1. In a large bowl, dissolve the yeast in ½ cup of the water. You can use water slightly warm from the faucet for this, but use cold water for the rest of the dough.

2. Once the yeast has dissolved, add the flour and then up to 1¼ cups of water. The dough should be soft and pliable. Let it rest for 10 minutes, and decide at that point whether or not to add the remaining ¼ cup of cold water.

3. Knead the dough in the bowl until it is smooth and soft. Rub a little oil on the dough and cover the bowl with a cloth for 30 minutes.

4. Once the dough has rested, you need to add air by kneading it for 5 minutes every 30 minutes. Do this three times.

5. At this stage, let the dough rise without touching it for 90 minutes in a warmish place in your kitchen.

6. Heat the oven to 400°F. Dust 2 baking sheets with flour or line them with parchment paper. Divide the dough into 2 pieces and gently press each piece out into a rectangular shape. Don't roll the dough or you will squeeze the air out of it. Irregularity in the dough is what you are striving for.

7. Drizzle the dough with olive oil and cover it with the topping of your choice— see some suggestions below. Bake for about 15 minutes, or until golden.

 TIPS

❖ Our favorite topping at the moment is potato & rosemary (pictured opposite). You will need olive oil, 2 baking potatoes (peeled and sliced ¹⁄₁₆ inch thick), 1 cup mascarpone cheese, 1 cup heavy cream, a sprig of fresh rosemary, and salt and pepper. Rub the dough with oil, arrange the potato slices on top, dot with the cheese, and pour over the cream. Scatter rosemary leaves over the top and season with salt and pepper.

❖ Other toppings we like:

   • Prosciutto, crème fraîche, sage
   • Halved cherry tomatoes, salami, mozzarella, finely chopped dried chili
   • Bulk sausage, fennel seed, crème fraîche, blanched broccoli
   • Stilton, walnut, endive, or other chicory

❖ Add about ½ cup sourdough starter (see page 195) to the dough to give it a wonderful sour flavour.

Oatmeal Cookies

These cookies are buttery and crumbly and the best thing to eat with a hard British cheese. Also wonderful spread with a nut butter (see page 57).

Makes: 12
Preparation time: 15 minutes +
30 minutes chilling time
Cooking time: 10 minutes
✓ V

2¾ cups **rolled oats**
1⅓ cups **spelt flour**, plus extra for dusting
1 cup **whole-grain spelt flour**
½ teaspoon **baking soda**
1 teaspoon **salt**
2¼ sticks **unsalted butter**
1 free-range **egg**

1. Mix together the oats, spelt flours, and baking soda. Rub the butter into the oats mixture between your fingertips until it just about disappears.

2. Add the salt and egg to bring the dough together, then chill for at least 30 minutes.

3. Meanwhile heat the oven to 350°F and line a baking sheet with parchment paper.

4. Roll out the dough to about ⅛ inch thickness on a lightly floured surface. Cut out the cookies with a round cutter, or cut a circle of dough 7 inches in diameter and then cut that into 4 wedges.

5. Place the cookies on the baking sheet and cook in the oven for 8–10 minutes. They will crisp up as they cool. They should be eaten fresh or kept in an airtight container for up to a week.

 TIPS

✤ These cookies will absorb moisture and become soft if left out, but they can be recrisped (as can any cookies containing butter) by laying them out on a baking sheet lined with parchment paper and putting them into a preheated oven at 325°F for 5 minutes.

✤ A Christmas essential with Stilton cheese.

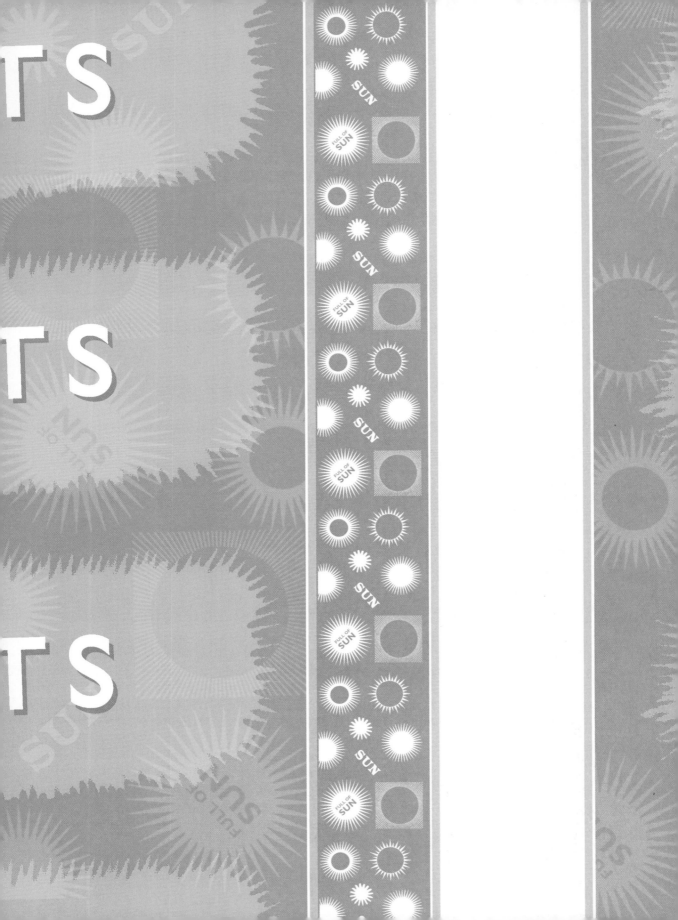

SWEETS

SWEETS

Somewhat like bread, mass-produced sweet treats have become so cheap and commonplace that people no longer even think of making them at home. This is a shame. There is a delicacy to the flavor of homemade treats and a beauty to their irregularity that cannot be reproduced in a factory. It is also a particular thrill to learn how to magic up your favorite confections: like becoming Willy Wonka for a day.

These recipes are simpler than they look, but allow yourself plenty of time to experiment. The alchemy of making your own sweet treats deserves to be savored.

CHOCOLATE MAKING DAY

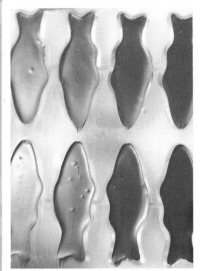

Strawberry Marshmallows

Homemade marshmallows—soft, oozing mouthfuls with little resemblance to the dried-out, spongy things you can buy in the supermarket. You don't have to use a sugar thermometer, but it makes things much simpler (and they are easy to buy online).

Makes: 20 marshmallows
Preparation time: 20 minutes
Cooking time: 30 minutes
❤ WF GF
(V if you use vegetarian gelatin)

¼ cup **confectioners' sugar**
¼ cup **cornstarch**
2 tablespoons **powdered gelatin**
6 tablespoons **water**
1 cup superfine **caster sugar**
1½ teaspoons **light corn syrup**
1 **free-range egg white**
½ cup pureed **strawberries**, strained (about 8oz whole berries)
1 teaspoon **vanilla extract**

1. Oil a 2¾ inch deep 9–10 inch roasting pan. Sift together the confectioners' sugar and cornstarch. Then, using about half the mixture, sift it over your oiled pan to coat.

2. Soften the gelatin in ¼ cup of cold water in a small saucepan, off the heat.

3. In another small saucepan, combine the superfine sugar, light corn syrup, and the remaining water and place over low heat. Stir to dissolve the sugar. Bring the syrup to a boil and insert a sugar thermometer. You want to heat the syrup to the "hard-ball" stage, 260°F.

4. While the sugar boils, work quickly and beat the egg white in a large bowl with an electric handheld mixer. Set aside.

5. Just before the syrup reaches hard-ball stage, place the softened gelatin in its water over low heat until it is dissolved. Now, with your syrup at hard-ball stage and the gelatin dissolved, remove from the heat and combine the two by pouring the gelatin mixture into the syrup and beating by hand.

6. Add the strawberry puree and the vanilla extract to the gelatin-sugar mixture.

7. Now pour the strawberry mixture into the egg whites in a slow, steady stream, beating as you pour, until all the mixture has been incorporated.

8. Beat on medium-high speed for 5 minutes, or until the mixture is thick and billowy. Pour into the prepared pan and smooth the top. Let set for about an hour.

9. Dust your work surface with more cornstarch and confectioners' sugar and turn the marshmallow out on to it. Cut into cubes and serve. Store in an airtight container for up to a week. (Dust again to stop the marshmallows from sticking together.)

TIPS

❖ These would be perfect to add to S'mores (see page 180).

Honeycomb Toffee

If this recipe that doesn't get your inner child hopping up and down with excitement, wait until you see what happens at the critical moment in this recipe. It's like the best chemistry lesson you never had.

Makes: an 8 x 8 inch pan
Preparation time: 5 minutes
Cooking time: 15 minutes
♥ WF GF V

1 stick **unsalted butter**
1 tablespoon **white wine vinegar**
1¼ cups **light corn syrup**
2 cups **superfine sugar**
1 teaspoon **baking soda**, sifted

1. Butter an 8 inch-square cake pan and line it with parchment paper.

2. Put a LARGE, heavy, saucepan (the size is very important) over low heat and melt the butter. Add the vinegar, corn syrup, and superfine sugar, letting the syrup and sugar melt into the butter. Turn the heat up to medium without stirring the mixture. Insert a sugar thermometer and heat the syrup until it reaches the "hard-crack" stage (300°F).

3. Remove the pan from the heat and immediately stir in the baking soda. The baking soda will fill the mixture with air bubbles of carbon dioxide so that it foams up dramatically, threatening to overflow, and engulf your kitchen. That's why you make it in a LARGE pan.

4. Pour the mixture into your prepared cake pan and let it cool. When it begins to set, score the honeycomb toffee with a knife into bite-size pieces. Once it is completely cooled, it can be broken into pieces along the score lines and stored in an airtight container.

TIPS

❖ Coat the honeycomb toffee with chocolate (see page 44 for how to temper it) to make your own candy bar.

❖ Otherwise, it's great crunched up into cake frostings, or sprinkled on top of a cake to give it a golden sparkle.

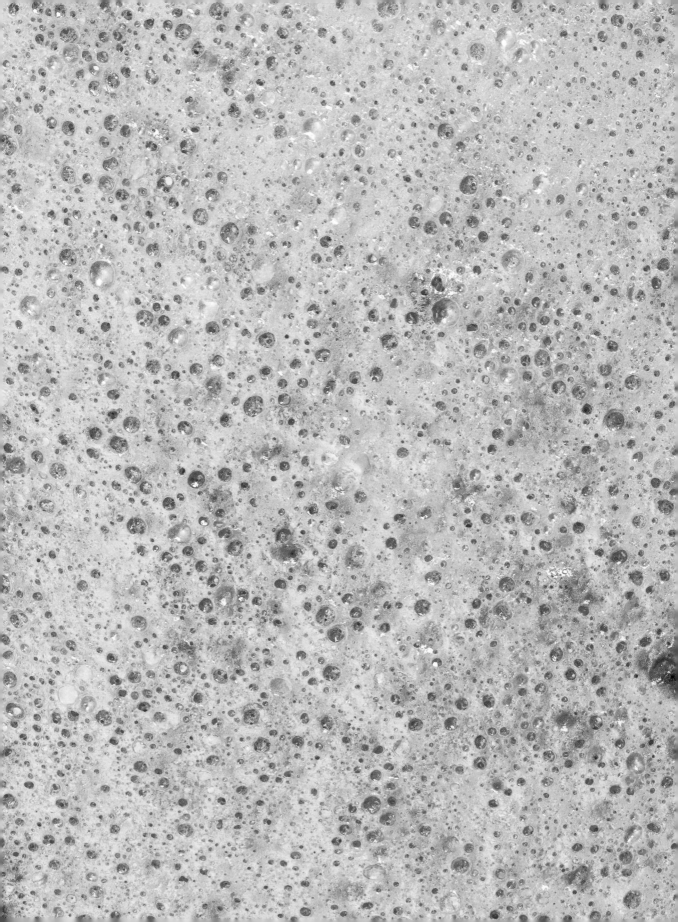

Soli's Floral Persian Dates (with Burned Almonds & Pistachios)

These are the daintiest treats you've ever seen: each one a beautifully wrapped package of sweetness. Popular all over the Middle East, they have been perfected by Claire's Iranian friend Soli.

Makes 25 (enough for about 8 people)
Preparation time: 30 minutes
Cooking time: none
♥ ✓ WF GF V

25 **Persian dates** (Medjool will do, but Persian dates are juicier)
13–14 **almonds**, cut in half lengthwise
¼ cup **mascarpone**
1½ teaspoons **confectioners' sugar**
3 tablespoons **orange blossom water**
25 **whole unsalted pistachios** (nice green ones!)
a handful of **dried rose petals**, to decorate

1. Start with the dates. Using a sharp knife, cut them lengthwise. Remove the stone from each one and gently push the cavity open.

2. Brown the almonds in a heavy skillet until they turn a nice, smoky, dark brown (but are not quite burned), then set aside.

3. Spoon the mascarpone into a small bowl. Gradually combine with the confectioners' sugar and orange blossom water, adding a little at a time, and pushing down with the back of the spoon until you have a smooth and fluffy mixture.

4. Using your smallest teaspoon, carefully stuff the cavity in each date with the orange blossom mascarpone.

5. Press half an almond and a whole pistachio into the top of each stuffed date, arrange on a platter, and scatter over rose petals. Serve with Persian black cardamom tea. Bah bah! (Persian for: yum yum!).

FRIENDS & FAMILY RECIPES

Soli in Dubai, 1988

Soli Zardosht has an adorable stall at Broadway Market in Hackney, east London, called Black Lime, named for the Persian spice that features heavily in the cooking of that region. She is a wonderful cook and wonderful host.

CLAIRE

JAMS & COMPOTES

SPECIAL FRUIT STANDARD

STRAWBERRY, RASPBERRY, QUINCE, DRIED FRUIT

From our first day at Leon, we have made our own jams and compotes because most commercial ones contain ridiculous amounts of sugar. We blend the compotes into our power smoothies as well as adding them to our yogurts for breakfast.

Compote is much the same as jam but the fruit tends to be less broken down and, unlike jam, it does not set. Both are great methods for making ripe fruit last a little bit longer. Compote will keep for a couple of weeks in an airtight jar in the refrigerator; jam should keep for a year at room temperature and then for a couple of months in the refrigerator once it is opened.

SERVE THE COMPOTES WITH CHEESE, OR WITH YOGURT FOR A LIGHT EVENING DESSERT; SPOON THEM OVER ICE CREAM; MIX A LITTLE INTO FRUIT SALAD; OR USE THEM JUST LIKE JAM—ON TOAST.

Fresh Strawberry Jam

Fresh jams like this one are so easy to make and taste wonderful. They are a very good way to use up overripe fruit.

Makes: 2½ cups
Preparation time: 3 hours
Cooking time: 10 minutes
❤ ✓ WF GF DF V

1lb **strawberries**, hulled and quartered
½ cup **agave nectar**

1. Soak the strawberries in the agave syrup for about 3 hours.

2. Place in a small nonreactive saucepan and bring to a boil. Boil for 7 minutes, then pour into a sterilized container. Check USDA guidelines for sterilizing and processing. Store in the refrigerator.

Fresh Raspberry Jam

This jam takes a mere 10 minutes to cook, but the fruit and sugar must macerate overnight to get the right consistency.

Makes: about 4 cups
Preparation time: 5 minutes
+ overnight macerating
Cooking time: 10 minutes
❤ WF GF DF V

4 cups **raspberries**
2½ cups **granulated sugar**
juice of 1 **lemon**

Irish chef Darina Allen taught me that jam should take only 5–7 minutes to cook on the stove in order that it should taste of the fresh fruit. It was an invaluable lesson and has changed the way I make jams.
CLAIRE

1. Place the raspberries and sugar in a bowl. Toss and let macerate overnight.

2. Place the mixture in a warm saucepan on the stove and stir gently. Once the fruit comes to a boil, cook for only 5–7 minutes.

3. Decant into a bowl (if you intend to eat it right away) or a couple of sterilized jars. The jam will set as it cools. Check USDA guidelines for processing.

TIPS

✤ Because of the high seed content in raspberries, they have a lot of natural pectin, which lets the jam set so beautifully. Other fruits can be made using this method but may need added pectin.

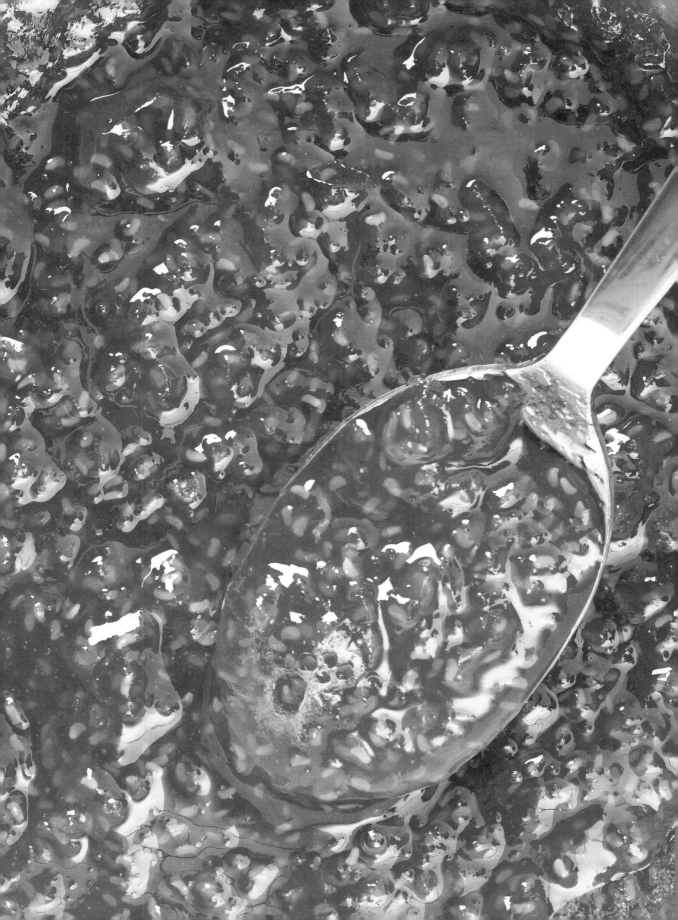

Roasted Quince Compote

Wonderful with cheese after dinner, and an awful lot easier than making membrillo (a traditional Spanish quince paste boiled for hours).

Makes: about 4 cups
Preparation time: 15 minutes
Cooking time: approx. 1 hour 40 minutes
♥ WF GF DF V

3 **quinces**
1 **bay leaf**
1 large strip of **lemon peel**
½ a **vanilla bean**, split in half lengthwise
1 cup **water**
1¼ cups **granulated sugar**

1. Heat the oven to 400°F.

2. Peel and quarter the quinces (don't worry about coring them until after they have been baked, when they are soft and easier to manage). Arrange them in a roasting pan large enough so that they have a little room.

3. Add the bay leaf, lemon peel, and vanilla bean and cover with water and sugar. Cover tightly with aluminum foil and bake for 1 hour.

4. Remove the foil, then reduce the oven temperature to 340°F, toss the quinces in the juices, and put the pan back in the oven for another 35–40 minutes. The compote is ready when it is a deep pinky red and the sugar syrup is thick.

5. Remove the cores from the quince when they have cooled and before you serve the compote.

TIPS

❖ Small pieces of the cooked quince can also be added to crisps and crumbles (see pages 128–133), or thinly sliced on a tart.

❖ Make a panna cotta or other creamy pudding and serve with the compote.

❖ Serve on top of a good yogurt for breakfast.

Dried Fruit Compote

Dried sour cherries and apricots provide a wonderful way to spruce up a winter dessert when other fruits are out of season. This compote is spicy, tart, and sweet. Use it alongside the Clementine Cornmeal Cake (page 89), or with a dollop of Greek yogurt for a simple dessert fit for a king.

Makes: about 4 cups
Preparation time: 5 minutes
Cooking time: 10 minutes, plus 30 minutes resting time
♥ WF GF DF V

1 cup **superfine sugar**
½ cup **water**
½ a stick of **cinnamon**
½ a **vanilla bean**, split in half lengthwise, seeds scraped
1 **orange**
1½ cups **quatrered dried apricots**
⅔ cup **dried sour cherries**

1. In a medium saucepan, combine the sugar, water, cinnamon, vanilla bean and seeds and the zest of half the orange. Bring the mixture slowly to a boil, stirring occasionally to dissolve the sugar.

2. Add the quartered apricots and the sour cherries to the boiling syrup. Add the juice of the whole orange. Stir, then remove the pan from the heat. Place a lid or plate over the pan and let the fruit steep for half an hour.

TIPS

❖ This compote is also great with oatmeal at breakfast.

❖ You could make this without the cinnamon and cherries for a vanilla and apricot compote.

❖ Add golden raisins and a cardamom pod for variation.

Dried Fruit Compote (above) and
Roasted Quince Compote (below)

Maggie Levinger and I are from the same small town in Northern California. She comes from a huge family (she has seven brothers and sisters), and I spent a lot of time at her house when I was growing up. One of Maggie's main hobbies was having bake sales in the town (something I also did). At a tender age, Maggie was already famous locally for her blackberry crisps and huckleberry pies.

Years later, after her mother was diagnosed with cancer, Maggie began to look for healthier alternatives to the sweet things that she grew up with. She studied whole-grain nutrition and worked as a chef at revolutionary raw food restaurants in California. She now runs Wild West Ferments in Marin County with her partner Luke—growing food, making sauerkraut, brining vegetables, and perfecting wild-fermented fruit sodas.

They both visited London recently and parked their camper van outside our flat for a week. It was perfect timing: I was in the middle of a "cleanse", and her knowledge of alternative foods, and "live" and raw food preparation, was a revelation. As they drove around Europe, they were growing sprouts and making wild-fermented fruit sodas right in their van.

Maggie has been a great help with some of the recipes in this book. She excels at baking and has an extensive knowledge of healthy, whole ingredients.

Maggie either conceived and/or contributed to Hazelnut and Pumpkin Seed Milks (page 56), Chocolate Hazelnut Power Pills (page 71), the Bar of Good Things (page 80), Chocolate Chip Cookies (page 184), and Coconut Kiss Ice Cream (page 170).

CLAIRE

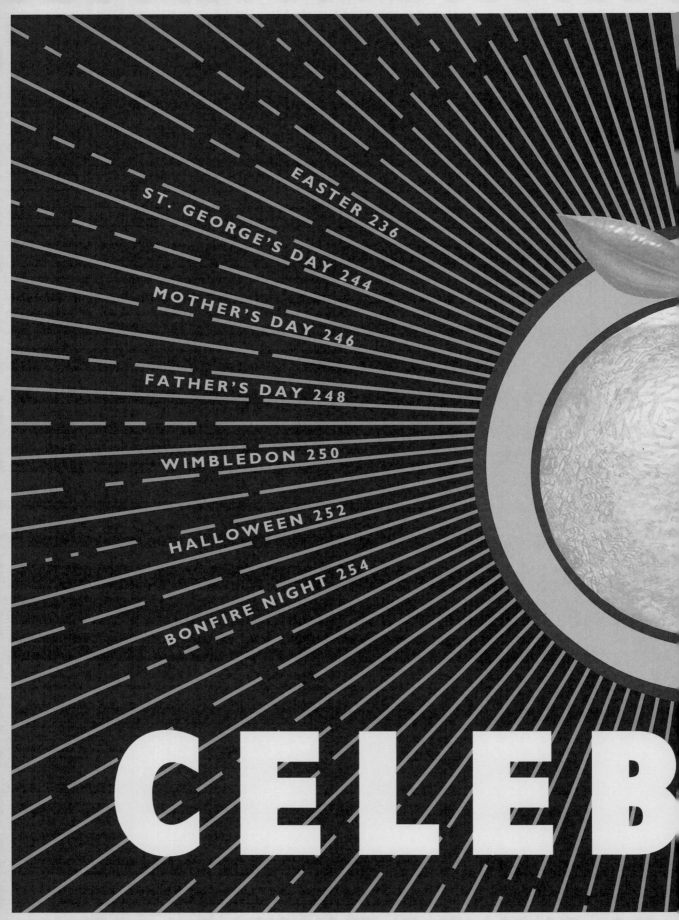

CELEB

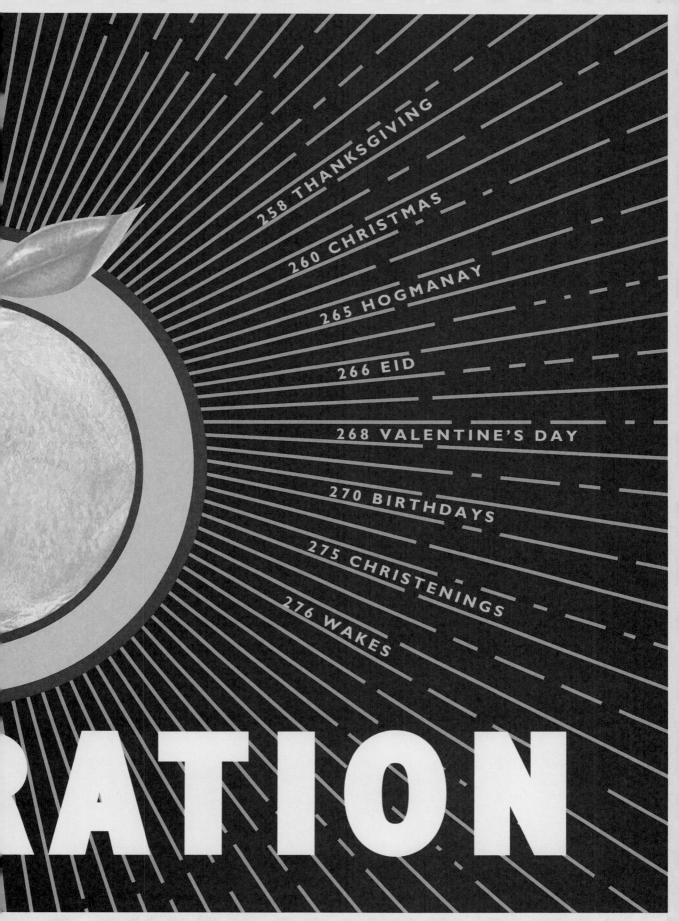

RATION

Spelt Pancakes

The key is to throw the pancakes as high as you can without getting them stuck to the ceiling.

Makes: approx. 20 pancakes
Preparation time: 1 hour 10 minutes
Cooking time: 3 minutes

♥ ✓ V

1 cup **white spelt flour**
a pinch of **salt**
1 **free-range egg**
¾ cup **whole milk**
3 tablespoons **ale** or **lager**
butter, for the skillet
lemon juice and **superfine sugar**, to serve

1. Put the flour into a large bowl and add the salt.

2. Beat in the egg from the center, moving outward in a clockwise motion.

3. Add the milk and beat to a smooth batter.

4. Strain the batter into a large measuring cup and stir in the beer. Chill the pancake batter for at least an hour.

5. Heat a nonstick skillet or iron crepe pan until hot, then add a little butter. Stir the batter a little before pouring a small amount into the skillet. Swirl the batter quickly around the skillet to coat in a thin, even layer.

6. Cook for a minute or so, until it starts to bubble, then slide a thin spatula beneath the pancake to loosen it and flip it over. Flip 'em high—that is the fun part. Cook for another minute or so before piling the pancakes up on a plate to cool.

7. To serve, squeeze lemon juice over the pancakes, sprinkle with sugar, then fold into triangles or roll into scrolls.

TIPS

❖ Letting the batter rest makes all the difference. Don't be tempted to skip that step.

❖ You can use agave nectar instead of superfine sugar. You can also substitute white flour for the spelt flour if you want to. And, of course, you can use water instead of beer.

Simnel Cake

This is another cake from the wonderful Petra (see page 274). Simnel cake is a British Easter tradition. It is widely accepted that the balls of marzipan on top are meant to represent the disciples, but there is some debate as to how many there should be: eleven if you exclude the traitor Judas, twelve if you count him in, or thirteen to include Jesus. Petra's homemade marzipan is so good that we recommend thirteen: every time you leave the room you will return to find that another ball has mysteriously vanished.

Serves: 10–12
Preparation time: 1 hour
Cooking time: 3½ hours

For the marzipan
3 cups **confectioners' sugar**
4¾ cups **almond meal**
2 **free-range eggs**
1 teaspoon **lemon juice**
1 teaspoon **almond extract**

For the cake
1¾ cups **all-purpose flour**
½ teaspoon **salt**
¼ teaspoon freshly grated **nutmeg**
½ teaspoon **ground cinnamon**
¼ teaspoon **allspice**
1½ sticks **unsalted butter**
¾ cup **demerara sugar** or **other raw sugar**
2 tablespoons **molasses**
3 **free-range eggs**
3 cups **dried currants**
2 cups **golden raisins**
⅔ cup good-quality **mixed peel**
zest and juice of 1 **lemon**
½ cup **almond meal**
⅔ cup **whole milk**
a little **apricot jam**
1 **free-range egg**, slightly beaten (for an egg wash)

1. First make the marzipan. Sift the confectioners' sugar into a bowl, then add the almond meal, eggs, lemon juice, and almond extract to taste. Add the extract slowly, and keep tasting because some brands are stronger than others. Form into a ball and knead lightly. Divide into 3 pieces and wrap each one tightly in plastic wrap until ready to use.

2. Heat the oven to 300°F. Butter and line a deep 8 inch cake pan with parchment paper.

3. Sift together the flour, salt, and spices and set aside.

4. In another bowl, cream the butter, sugar, and molasses until very light and fluffy. Add the eggs, one at a time, sprinkling in a little of the sifted flour and beating well after each addition. Stir in the remaining flour, then the fruit, peel, zest, juice, and almond meal. Add the milk and mix until all the ingredients are well combined.

5. Roll out one of the pieces of marzipan into an 8 inch circle. Turn half the cake batter into the pan, level it out, and cover it with this circle of marzipan. Then cover with the rest of the cake batter and smooth the top.

6. Bake in the oven for about 3½ hours, or until a toothpick inserted comes out clean. The top of the cake should be dull, not shiny.

7. When the cake is cool, brush the top with a little warmed preserve, strained if necessary. Roll out another ball of marzipan and place it on top of the cake, pressing it down well. Score the top in a crosshatch pattern. Brush with egg wash.

8. Turn the broiler or oven to high. Divide the remaining ball of marzipan into 11 balls (representing the 12 apostles less Judas) and arrange them around the edge of the cake. Brush each ball with the egg wash and put the cake into the oven or under the broiler for a few minutes to give it that attractive, toasted appearance.

 TIPS

❖ Petra says the bore of Simnel cake is twiggy dried currants. She always picks them over to remove the little twigs.

❖ If your oven runs hot, wrap a second layer of paper around the perimeter of the cake pan to keep it from getting too dark.

❖ If you are serving the cake to the infirm, try to find pasteurized eggs—or eggs from flocks you trust for making the marzipan.

Spelt Hot Cross Buns

Wholesome and delicious. These buns are a little less sweet than most hot cross buns but just as festive. Toast them and slather with butter—or coconut oil if you don't do dairy. You can make the dough the day before, put them into the refrigerator overnight, and bake them fresh in the morning on Easter Day.

Makes: 12
Preparation time: 50 minutes +
3½–3¾ hours rising time
Cooking time: 15 minutes
♥ ✓ DF V

2 x (14oz) envelopes of **dry active yeast**
1 cup **rice milk**, warmed slightly, plus extra to brush the tops
1 cup **agave nectar**
2¼ cups **whole-grain spelt flour**
2¼ cups **spelt flour**
1 teaspoon **salt**
½ teaspoon **ground allspice**
½ teaspoon freshly grated **nutmeg**
1 teaspoon **ground cinnamon**
½ cup **dried currants**
½ cup **golden raisins**
zest of 1 **orange**
1 **free-range egg** or **egg substitute**
¼ cup **coconut oil**, melted

For the crosses:
⅔ cup **spelt flour**
1 tablespoon **water**

For the bun wash:
⅓ cup **water**
½ cup **agave nectar**

One a penny,
two a penny...

1. Preheat the oven to 425°F and line 2 baking sheets with parchment paper.

2. Dissolve the yeast in the warm rice milk with the agave nectar and set aside.

3. In a separate bowl, combine the flours, salt, spices, currants, and golden raisins and orange zest.

4. Add the egg or egg substitute and the coconut oil to the milk mixture, then pour all of this over the dry ingredients. Stir the dough to combine and then let it rest for about 20 minutes.

5. Turn the dough out onto a floured surface and knead it for 10–12 minutes, until it becomes silky. Put it back into the bowl and cover with a clean cloth. Let rest in a warm place until the dough has nearly doubled in bulk. This should take about 3 hours.

6. Divide the dough into 12 pieces. Form each piece into a ball and place on the prepared baking sheets, about 1 inch apart. Let the buns to rise on sheets for about 30–45 minutes, while you prepare the crosses.

7. When the buns have risen, brush them with a little rice milk. Put the ⅔ cup of flour for the crosses into a small bowl and add about 1 tablespoon of water to make a paste. Use a pastry bag with a small round tip (or make one out of paper), to pipe the paste in crosses over each bun. Bake in the oven for about 15 minutes, or until golden brown.

8. While the rolls are baking, make the "bun wash" by heating the water and agave nectar in a small saucepan.

9. As soon as the buns come out of the oven, brush them with the bun wash. Serve warm or toasted, with your favorite spreads.

EASTER EGGS

Mastering the art of tempering chocolate (see page 44) opens up a whole new world of Easter activities.

If you have the time and the resources, it is an easy next step to invest in a few molds and colorings and spend a day making your own Easter eggs. You can paint patterns or pictures onto the molds before filling them with chocolate. Children, especially, love designing their own eggs.

WARNING: IT CAN GET VERY MESSY.

Eccles Cakes

These Lancashire currant cakes are a quintessentially English treat. But only eat one: they are so rich that they were banned by the Puritans lest they agitate ungodly humors.

Makes: 12
Preparation time: 15 minutes +
1 hour chilling
Cooking time: 25 minutes

V

9 tablespoons **unsalted butter**
1½ cups firmly packed **dark brown sugar**
3 cups **dried currants**
2 teaspoons **ground cinnamon**
½ teaspoon **nutmeg**, freshly grated
zest of 1 **orange**
13oz ready-to-bake **puff pastry**, thawed if frozen
1 **free-range egg** or **egg yolk**, for glazing
1 tablespoon **light cream**

1. Melt the butter with the sugar, currants, cinnamon, nutmeg, and orange zest.

2. Chill for at least 1 hour, then divide the mixture into 12 balls.

3. Roll out the pastry and cut into 4 inch squares. Place a ball of filling on each one, then bring the edges together around the ball of filling and pinch to seal so the filling does not escape when cooking.

4. Place, seam side down, on a lined baking sheet and chill for 10 minutes. Heat the oven to 350°F.

5. In a small bowl, mix together the egg or egg yolk and cream with a fork to make an egg wash. Brush the cakes with the egg wash, then use scissors to snip 3 small holes in the top of each pastry. Bake in the oven for about 20–25 minutes, until golden and risen. Transfer to a wire rack to cool.

TIPS

✤ These are amazing served with a crumbly, mild Lancashire cheese. Hence the saying taught to us by Fred (below): "An Eccles cake without the cheese is like a kiss without the squeeze."

✤ Try adding a drop of rum to the currant mixture—a trick apparently used to help preserve them when the Lancastrians exported them in the early nineteenth century.

FRED LOSES HIS FIRST TOOTH, 1975

It isn't just the English who celebrate St. George's day. He also happens to be the patron saint of Malta, Ethiopia, Georgia, and Catalonia. However, don't let that stop you enjoying a quiet moment of British national pride, and a cake.

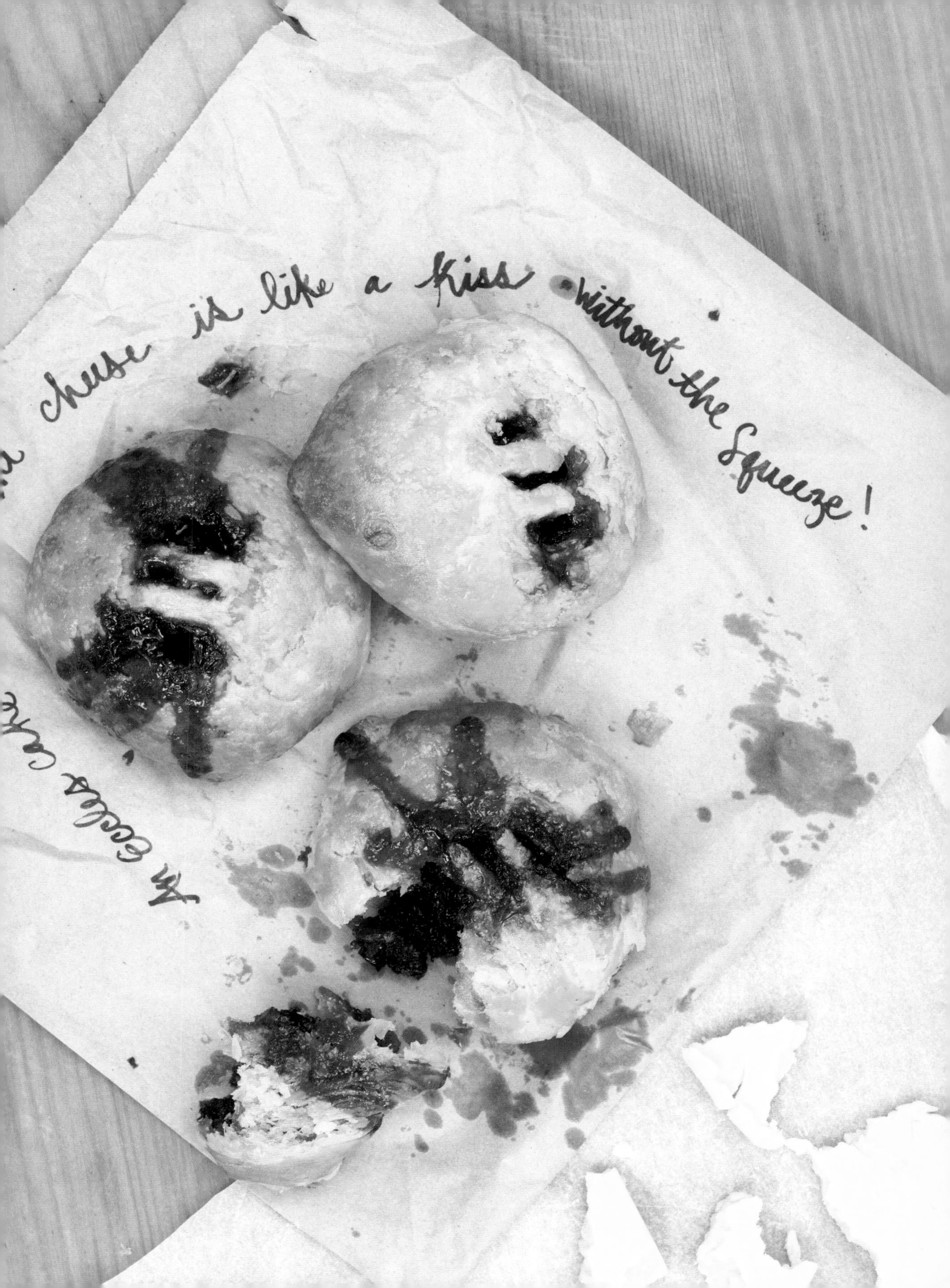
An Eccles cake
cheese is like a Kiss without the Squeeze!

Bill Granger's Scrambled Eggs on Spelt Toast

This is one of those recipes that manages to be easier and better than the traditional version—which involves cooking the eggs painfully slowly to make them creamy. Bill's method is similar to making a pancake, except that you mix it before it sets. Serve it on a couple of pieces of buttered spelt toast (see page 193) and your mother (or the mother of your children) will be eternally grateful.

Serves: 1 deserving woman on
Mothers' Day (generously)
Preparation time: 2 minutes
Cooking time: 5 minutes
✓ WF GF

2 really good **free-range eggs**
⅓ cup **heavy cream**
1 pinch of **salt**
1 tablespoon **unsalted butter**

1. Place the eggs, cream, and salt in a bowl and beat together.

2. Melt the butter in a nonstick skillet over high heat, being careful not to burn it.

3. Pour in the egg mixture and cook for 20 seconds, or until gently set around the edges.

4. Stir the eggs with a wooden spoon, gently bringing the egg mixture on the outside of the skillet to the center.

5. The idea is to fold the eggs instead of scrambling them.

6. Let cook for another 20 seconds and repeat the folding process.

7. When the eggs are just set (remembering that they will continue cooking as they rest), turn out onto a plate and serve with hot toast.

TIPS

❖ If you are making more than 2 servings of scrambled eggs, make sure you cook separate batches to avoid crowding the skillet.

❖ Bill uses milk instead of cream when he cooks them day to day. However, that seems a shame.

Bill Granger is a devilishly handsome Australian chef with a smile that would power a whole city. I was lucky enough to do a food demonstration with him at the Abergavenny food festival in Wales, where he taught me how to make these eggs. He discovered this method by chance while trying to make scrambled eggs too fast in his restaurant in Sydney—another great culinary accident.

HENRY

FRIENDS & FAMILY RECIPES

Bill in Melbourne, 1977

Glenys's Desperate Dan Steak Pie

Henry's next-door neighbor, Glenys, serves this simple steak pie to her man when she wants to treat him right. Cowboy horns optional.

Serves: 6
Preparation time: 20 minutes +
cooling time
Cooking time: 2¾ hours

olive oil or **vegetable oil**
3lb **chuck beef**, diced
6 **onions**, chopped
8 **bay leaves**
3¾ cups **Newcastle Brown Ale**, or a **similar sweet ale**
sea salt and **freshly ground black pepper**
13oz **ready-to-bake puff pastry**, thawed if frozen
   (or 1 quantity **flaky pie dough** from page 38)
1 **free-range egg**, beaten, for glazing

1. Heat the oven to 325°F.

2. Heat a dash of oil in a large casserole. Add the beef, brown on all sides, and set aside—you might need to do this in batches.

3. Add a dash more oil to the casserole, add the onions, and cook until golden.

4. Add the bay leaves and return the meat to the casserole.

5. Add the ale and season well with salt and pepper.

6. Cook in the oven for 2 hours, stirring every 45 minutes or so and checking that it hasn't dried out. You can add more ale if need be.

7. When the meat is tender, take out of the oven, let it cool, and taste for seasoning.

8. When you are ready to assemble the pie, heat the oven to 325°F. Transfer the cooled meat mixture to a pie plate and top with the ready-to-bake puff pastry. Press the pastry around the rim to seal. If you are feeling creative, try making a cow's head from the leftover pieces of pastry, or some horns. The children can help.

9. Glaze the top of the pastry with the beaten egg, using a pastry brush.

10. Bake for 40 minutes, or until the pastry is golden and you can see the juices bubbling up.

TIPS

❖ You can make the beef and ale filling well in advance of assembling it with the pastry.

❖ Double up on quantities and freeze half. Then you only need to defrost it if you want to make the pie in a hurry.

❖ You can add mushrooms and/or a can of diced tomatoes as an alternative.

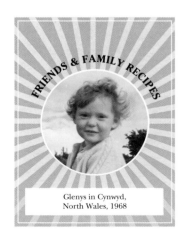

Glenys in Cynwyd,
North Wales, 1968

DESPERATE DAN PIE

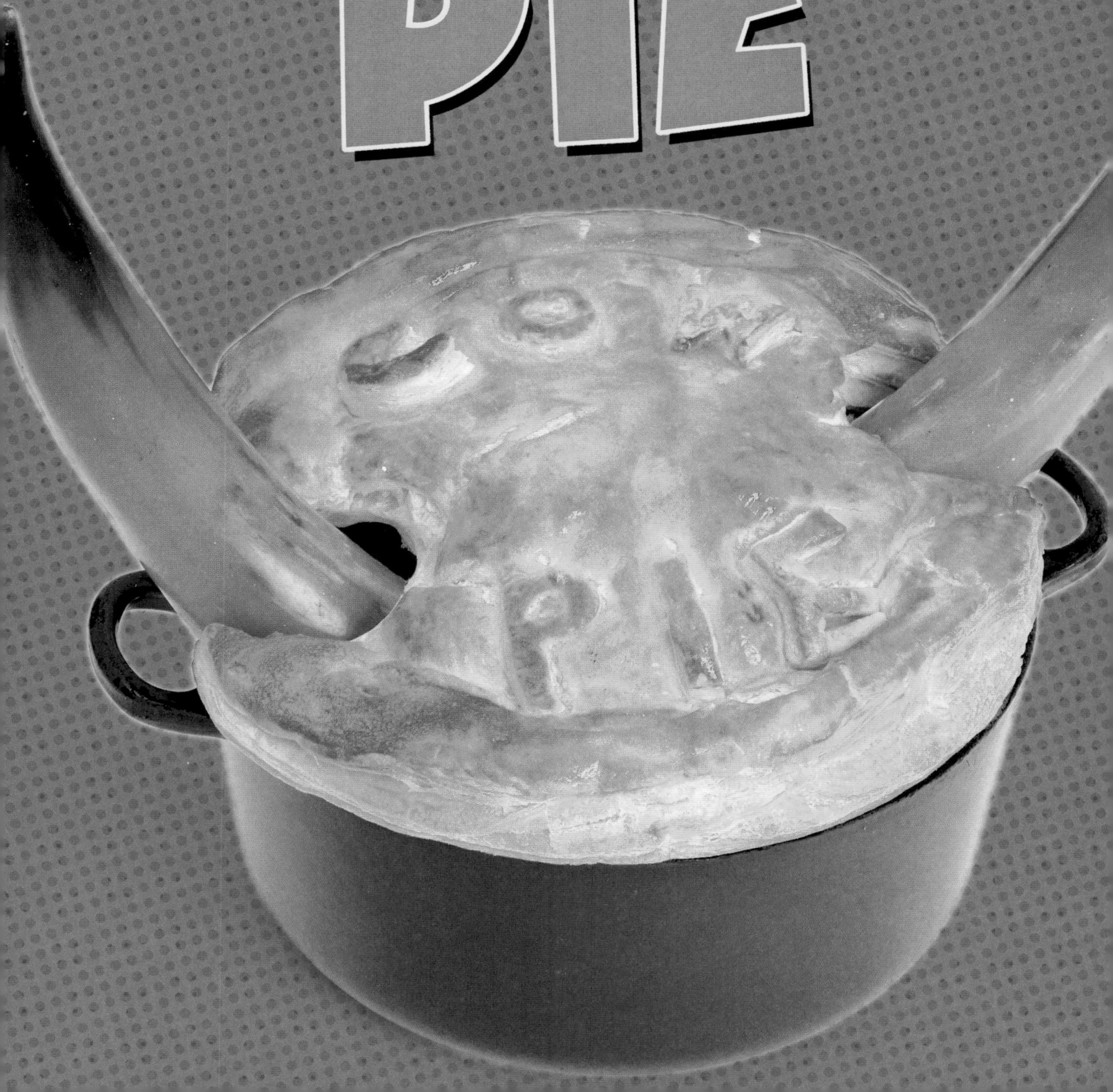

Bruno's Poached Strawberries with Green Peppercorn Ice Cream

People go on about how good strawberries are with pepper – and they are – but without sugar and cream they always seem to be a bit underdressed. This dish, created by chef Bruno Loubet, combines all three. It is sensational. Serve it to friends coming round to watch the Wimbledon final and they will remember it for ever.

Serves: 4
Preparation time: 2 hours
Freezing time: 1–3 hours
WF GF V

For the strawberries:
1 pint of **strawberries**
1 cup **water**
½ cup **caster sugar**

For the ice cream:
3 **free-range egg yolks**
¼ cup **superfine sugar**
½ cup **whole milk**
½ cup **heavy cream**
½ **vanilla bean** or 1½ teaspoons **vanilla extract**
2 teaspoons **green peppercorns** in brine, drained and dried
1 teaspoon **light corn syrup**

Bruno Loubet was my first boss. At the time, he was head chef at the Four Seasons on Hyde Park Corner, the first hotel in Great Britain to have a Michelin star restaurant. I was a lowly commis chef. Bruno always seemed to stand just the right side of the fine line between pride and arrogance. We were ferociously loyal to him. He is also one of the most creative chefs of his generation. This is just one of his beautiful creations.

HENRY

1. Put half of the strawberries into a blender or food processor and blend until smooth. Press through a strainer to make a coulis and set aside.

2. Combine the water and sugar in a saucepan and heat, stirring to dissolve the sugar. Bring to a boil and boil for 2 minutes, then pour the syrup into a bowl. Add the remaining strawberries and the strawberry coulis and stir gently to mix.

3. Set a plate on top to be sure the strawberries are completely immersed in the syrup, then let cool. When cold, refrigerate.

4. In a large bowl, mix together the egg yolks and sugar with a whisk until you obtain a white, creamy consistency.

5. Put the milk, cream, and vanilla bean into a heavy saucepan (if using vanilla extract, add it at the end). Heat until the milk boils and rises in the pan, then remove from the heat and pour the milk over the egg-sugar mixture, beating continuously. Return the mixture to the saucepan and cook on moderate heat, stirring continuously with a wooden spoon, until the cream thickens and will coat the back of a wooden spoon. Don't let the cream boil.

FRIENDS & FAMILY RECIPES

Bruno and his dog, 1969

6. Strain quickly through a fine strainer into a cold bowl. If using vanilla extract, add it now. When the custard is cold, cover and refrigerate.

7. Put the chilled custard into a blender and add the peppercorns and corn syrup. Process until fairly smooth. Alternatively, you can use an immersion blender. Pour into an ice cream machine and freeze according to the manufacturer's instructions.

8. With a slotted spoon, remove the strawberries from their syrup and put into a clean bowl. Strain the syrup through a strainer over the berries.

9. To serve, place scoops of the ice cream into pretty bowls. Divide the strawberries and syrup among the bowls.

TIPS

This is a good thing to make a day ahead, because the strawberries will benefit from a longer steeping and you will be too excited by the tennis to want to be toiling over the stove.

Halloween Cookies

Using the recipe for cookies on page 176, add either half a teaspoon of apple pie spice to make some lightly spiced cookies or substitute ⅔ cup unsweetened cocoa powder for ½ cup flour to make them chocolatey.

> *For each color icing:*
> **confectioners' sugar**
> 1 tablespoon of **water**
> a few drops of **food coloring**, colors of your choice
> **writing icing tubes**, for drawing

1. Make a few colored icings in different bowls by mixing together the confectioners' sugar, water, and food coloring until the icing is thick and smooth (but not too runny).

2. Using the icings as backgrounds and the writing icing tubes for the detail, unleash the creative beast in you.

ANITA (RIGHT) AND BRIDGET, WILLOUGHBY HALL, NOTTINGHAM UNIVERSITY, 1987

MATT (RIGHT) AND NEIL, WALLINGTON, 1981

Anita makes these cookies with her family every Halloween. She and her husband Matt start off decorating them with the kids, but when they're tucked up in bed, Anita and Matt carry on into the night attempting to make each other laugh with more and more ghoulish and ridiculous efforts. A perfect night of entertainment "for the kids".

HENRY

HALLOWEEN

Butterscotch Apples

This is a softer, gooier kind of caramel apple—a little easier on the teeth.

Makes: 6
Preparation time: 5 minutes
Cooking time: 10 minutes +
15 minutes cooling time
WF GF V

6 medium **apples**
6 tablespoons **unsalted butter**
¾ cup **superfine sugar**
2 tablespoons **light brown sugar**
½ cup **heavy cream**
½ cup **light corn syrup**
a pinch of **salt**
you will also need **wooden dowels**, ½ inch thick

1. Wash and dry your apples and push a dowel into the stem (top) end of each one. Line a baking sheet with parchment paper.

2. Put the butter, superfine sugar, brown sugar, cream, and corn syrup into a small heavy saucepan over medium heat, and stir to dissolve everything together into an emulsified mass.

3. Once the mixture has dissolved, bring it to a boil and cook until it reaches a light golden color.

4. Remove the caramel from the heat, quickly stir in the salt, then stop the cooking process by plunging the bottom of the pan into a sink full of ice-cold water and place the pan on a trivet to cool. Let the caramel cool for 15 minutes (this helps to stop it from sliding down the sides).

5. Dip the apples into the caramel, holding them by their sticks. Place the dipped apples on the prepared baking sheet and let them cool and set.

TIPS

❖ If the caramel starts to slip off of the apples, let them cool slightly and dip them again.

Mulled Wine

Spicy and sweet, but with clear flavors that aren't muddy.

Makes: 6½ cups
Preparation time: 5 minutes
Cooking time: 10 minutes
♥ WF GF DF V

2 bottles of **dry red wine**
1 cup **superfine sugar**
1 stick of **cinnamon**
2 **cloves**
1 **star anise**
1 piece of **lemon peel**
1 piece of **orange peel**, plus extra to serve

1. Pour the wine into a large saucepan. Add the sugar and spices. Heat wine over a medium heat. Do not let it boil but heat it through so that it is steaming and the spices have a chance to steep. Add the lemon and orange peels, using a vegetable peeler to get nice wide pieces.

2. Simmer the wine for about 10 minutes, stirring occasionally, making sure the sugar has dissolved.

3. Serve with a twist of orange.

 TIPS

❖ If you are out of oranges but have clementines, use them.

❖ This is even better with a generous glug of brandy.

❖ This mulled wine is not too sweet (how we like it), but you can add more sugar if you prefer it sweeter.

 I came up with this recipe at Henry and Mima's house, when they were hosting a neighborhood Christmas party. They have a wonderful collection of whole spices in their kitchen, so it was a cinch. The last of the neighbors staggered out at 2 a.m., pretty well spiced themselves.

CLAIRE

Pumpkin Pie

A warm, deeply spicy version of this Thanksgiving classic.

Serves: 8–10
Preparation time: 25 minutes
Cooking time: 35 minutes
♥ V

2 cups fresh or 1 x (15oz) can **pumpkin purée**
3 **free-range eggs**
½ cup **heavy cream**
⅔ cup **light brown sugar**
1 teaspoon **ground cinnamon**
½ teaspoon **ground ginger**
½ teaspoon **ground star anise**
½ teaspoon **ground allspice**
1 teaspoon **sea salt**
3 tablespoons **maple syrup**
finely grated **fresh ginger** (optional)
black pepper (optional
1 x quantity **Flaky Pie Dough** (see page 38) or
    1 x (9 inch) ready-to-bake pie shell

1. Heat the oven to 350°F.

2. Beat all the ingredients together, except the fresh ginger, in a large bowl. The pie will be silkier if the pumpkin is as smooth as possible, so pour the filling through a fine strainer (even if you have pushed your puree through one initially).

3. Taste the filling. At this point, you can add a little finely grated fresh ginger, along with a good grinding of black pepper to taste.

4. Roll out the dough, if using, as thinly as possible and press into a 9 inch fluted tart pan with a loose bottom, then trim the edges. Pour the filling into the pie shell and bake in the oven for about 35 minutes, or until the custardy filling is just set while retaining a slight wobble.

5. Cool and serve with a lot of Chantilly cream (heavy cream sweetened with superfine sugar and a dash of vanilla extract).

(TIPS)

✤ To make your own puree, cut a small cooking pumpkin in half and bake it in a hot oven, cut side down. When it is soft, scrape out the center and puree.

✤ If the pumpkins are not as sweet as you'd like, some freshly pureed butternut squash will help. If you don't happen to have that, a little extra sugar will do.

Thanksgiving is sacred to ua because it is a holiday free from the pressures of gift giving, and is all about breaking bread with family and friends and often strangers. This recipe was published on the *Guardian*'s Allotment Blog after I made it for a Thanksgiving dinner celebrated with several other Americans living in Great Britain.

CLAIRE

Kamal's Meghli

This sweet, scented Lebanese rice pudding is traditionally served at Christmas or to celebrate the birth of a child. We were taught it by our friend Kamal Mouzawak, a celebrated Lebanese cook.

Serves 8
Preparation time: soaking the nuts overnight
Cooking time: 30 minutes
♥ WF GF DF V

⅓ cup **whole almonds**, skins on
⅓ cup **pistachios**
7½ cups **water**
1 cup **rice flour**
1½ cups **sugar**
1 tablespoon **caraway seeds**
1½ teaspoons **ground cinnamon**
1½ teaspoons **ground anise seeds**

Kamal at home in Jeita, Christmas Day, 1975

1. Soak the almonds and the pistachios in water, in separate bowls, overnight. Peel and halve them the next day.

2. Boil 6¾ cups of water in a medium saucepan. Put the rice flour, sugar and spices into a bowl and add the remaining water. Mix well, then add to the boiling water, stirring continuously.

3. Reduce the heat, stir well, then bring to a boil again. Let the mixture cook until it thickens. Stir continuously with a wooden spoon so the rice doesn't stick to the bottom of the pan—this will take about 20 minutes.

4. Pour into individual serving bowls and let cool. Before serving, garnish each bowl with almonds and pistachios.

The centerpieces of my grandparents' Christmases were meghli—to eat—ar the Adonis Gardens—for decoration. Meghli is traditionally served to celebrate the birth of a new baby, and prepared by the two grandmas (one more thing for them to compete over) In the mountain regions, it has also become a Christmas treat, in honor o Jesus's birth. It is said that the brown pudding symbolizes a fertile, rich soi and the nuts on the top are seeds that will sprout and grow.

The Adonis Gardens (see picture opposite) is a traditional homemade nativity scene, decorated with sprouts. On Berbera (our equivalent of Halloween, on December 5), we woul put together the tableau showing the infant Christ in a cave, add layers of wet cottonballs and plant them with seeds (wheat, lentils, chickpeas). By Christmas, the seeds would have sproute into tiny fields of green. As the name suggests, it is one of those Christmas traditions that actually has pagan roo it was originally done by Athenean women to celebrate the life cycle of the god Adonis, who was said to com from Phoenicia (now Lebanon).

KAMAL

Jossy's Orange Mincemeat Pies

My mom, Josceline Dimbleby, wrote the first British supermarket cook book about Christmas. It sold hundreds of thousands of copies. Wherever I go, I meet people who tell me that they still cook her mince pies and Christmas pudding. They are wonderful recipes. HENRY

Makes: 24
Preparation time: 40 minutes
Cooking time: 20 minutes
V

4 cups **all-purpose flour**
  or 4½ cups **spelt flour**
1¼ cups **superfine sugar**
3¼ sticks **unsalted butter**, diced
finely grated zest and juice of
  1 **large orange**
vegetable oil, for greasing
1 cup **cream cheese**
1¾–2¼ cups good-quality **mincemeat**
milk, to glaze
confectioners' sugar, to decorate

I devised these pies years ago, and they have proved to be one of my most popular recipes. The addition of cream cheese is optional, but by mixing it with the spicy mincemeat you can give them a really luxurious texture.

JOSSY

1. Sift the flour and 1 cup of superfine sugar into a mixing bowl, then rub in the butter with your fingers until the mixture resembles bread crumbs.

2. Stir in the orange zest, then the juice using a knife, until the pastry just begins to stick together. Gather up the pastry and pat it into a ball with lightly floured hands. Wrap it in clingfilm and chill it in the fridge for at least 30 minutes.

3. Preheat the oven to 400°F. Grease two 12-cup mini muffin pans.

4. Beat together the cream cheese and ¼ cup superfine sugar in a bowl until smooth.

5. Remove the dough from the refrigerator. Knead it lightly, then divide it in half and roll out one half more thickly than usual. Using an 3 inch pastry cutter, cut out 24 circles, rerolling the dough as necessary.

6. Line the muffin pans with the dough circles. Fill to half their depth with mincemeat, then put a teaspoon of the cream cheese mixture on top and smooth it level.

7. Roll out the remaining dough, and using a 2 inch pastry cutter (or star-shaped cutter like we did), cut another 24 circles. Moisten the underside of the circles with milk, water, or beaten egg, and place them on top of the filled pies. Press the edges together lightly and make a small slit in the top of each pie.

8. Brush the tops with milk and bake in the oven for 15–20 minutes, until golden.

9. Ket the mincemeat pies to cool slightly before removing them from the pans, then sprinkle with confectioners' sugar. Serve warm or cold.

TIPS

❖ To make the pastry even more crumbly, use two-thirds butter and one-third lard or vegetable shortening.

❖ Mincemeat can be greatly improved by adding lemon juice and some finely chopped sharp apple.

Jossy's Favourite Round Christmas Pudding

This is the classic version of Jossy's Christmas pudding. If you want to make it wheat and gluten free, simply substitute the bread crumbs with cooked basmati rice or gluten-free bread crumbs.

Serves 8–10
Preparation time: 1 hour
Cooking time: 6 hours
❤ ✓ DF V

2¾ cups **pitted prunes**

1¼ cups **crystallized ginger**

⅓ cup **walnut halves**

1½ cups large **raisins**

grated zest and juice of 2 **oranges**

3 cups **whole-wheat bread crumbs**

⅔ cup **shredded vegetable suet**

¼ teaspoon **ground cloves**

3 large **free-range eggs**

2–3 tablespoons **Cointreau** or **brandy**

1. Generously butter the two halves of a circular mold, 2-quart deep, round, ovenproof bowl or aluminum foil-lined rice steamer.

2. Cut the prunes into fairly small pieces and coarsely chop the ginger and walnuts. Put the chopped ingredients into a large bowl with the raisins, orange zest, bread crumbs, suet, and ground cloves.

3. In another bowl, beat the eggs until frothy and slightly thickened and stir well into the dry ingredients. Lastly stir in the orange juice and the Cointreau or brandy.

4. Let stand for half an hour or more, to let the ingredients blend together. If you are using a mold, spoon the mixture into both halves, filling them completely and spreading level. Close the halves to form the circle and wrap thoroughly with more foil. Put a metal cookie cutter in the bottom of a large saucepan and stand the mold on top. Pour in enough boiling water to come three-quarters of the way up the side of the mold. Then cover the pan and steam gently for about 6 hours, checking now and then and adding more boiling water if it has evaporated at all.

5. If you are using an ovenproof bowl, fill it to the top and smooth it level. Cover the bowl with parchment paper and then a layer of foil, and tie string tightly just under the lip of the bowl. Trim it well so that the foil and paper do not dangle in the water and place the bowl in a saucepan. Fill the pan with water to come halfway up the side of the bowl, and simmer as instructed above, filling up the water levels every now and then.

6. When the pudding is cold, keep it in a cool place until Christmas Day. Then put it into a saucepan as before and steam for another hour or so before serving. Serve on a warmed plate, stick a sprig of holly on top, pour bubbling Cointreau or brandy around the pudding, and set it alight as you approach the festive table.

Over the years, I have made countless variatio of Christmas pudding a we all think this beats them all. With squidgy prunes, walnuts, and a tang of fresh orange, it dark, full of flavor, and gooey, yet crumbly and light because it contain flour or sugar. People h been known to eat three helpings at one sitting, and even children like i the fruit makes it sweet enough. You can now b metal molds to make de round puddings, but I st use a large Chinese rice steamer that I line with aluminum foil. Of cour if you haven't got a mo you can always make th pudding in a deep, roun 2-quart ovenproof bowl You don't have to make this pudding months in advance.

JOSSY

Champagne Cocktail

A drink to toast the New Year—in Scotland this is called Hogmany.

Serves: 1
Preparation time: 2 minutes
Cooking time: none
♥ ✓ WF GF DF V

Also voluntarily tested by
Anita, Georgia, Issy, and Apple

Angostura bitters
1 sugar cube
brandy
Champagne

1. Shake a couple of drops of Angostura onto the sugar cube and put it into the bottom of a Champagne glass.

2. Pour on a little brandy. It is meant to be just a dash, but they say that fortune favors the bold.

3. Fill up the glass with Champagne.

TIPS

❖ You can use cava or prosecco or any dry sparkling white wine instead of Champagne (we normally do).

❖ If you don't like brandy, you can omit it. The original recipe doesn't include it.

Turkish Delight

Eid ul-Fitr
(festivity at the end of the fast)
is the three-day Muslim festival
that ends Ramadan.

These quivering little rose water gelatins are sweet, but with strong tea or coffee at the end of a feast they will perk you right up. They are eaten to celebrate Eid across the Middle East, as well as by the Turkish community in Dalston, where we both live.

Makes: 30 squares
Preparation time: 10 minutes +
cooling time
Cook time: 40 minutes
❤ ✓ WF GF DF V

2¼ cups **superfine sugar**
3¾ cups **water**
a pinch of **cream of tartar**
¾ cup **cornstarch**
1⅔ cups **confectioners' sugar**
2 teaspoons **rose water**
    or 1 teaspoon **lemon oil**
pink food coloring (optional)
⅓ cup **confectioners' sugar**,
    plus ⅓ cup **cornstarch**,
    for dusting

1. Grease an 8–9 inch square cake pan or similar, and line with parchment paper.

2. In a medium saucepan, dissolve the superfine sugar, ½ cup of the water and the cream of tartar (the acidity of the cream of tartar stops the sugar from crystallizing). Stir to dissolve, then bring to a boil. Boil for 5 minutes, then turn off the heat.

3. In a large bowl, combine the ¾ cup of cornstarch, 1⅔ cups confectioners' sugar and ¼ cup of water to make a paste. Boil the remaining 3 cups of water and gradually beat it into the cornstarch paste. This is an important step in order to avoid lumps.

4. Transfer the cornstarch mixture to a large saucepan and place over medium heat. Simmer the mixture until thickened and nearly translucent.

5. Take the pan off the heat and gradually pour in the sugar syrup, beating continuously. Turn the heat down slightly and boil for 30 minutes, until yellowish and thick.

6. Add the rose water or lemon oil and a few drops of pink coloring (if using) and pour into the pan. Let cool completely. This could take overnight.

7. In a bowl, sift together the confectioners' sugar and cornstarch for dusting. Cut the Turkish delight into cubes and toss in the sugar-cornstarch mixture.

TIPS

❖ Dip the pieces of Turkish delight in chocolate for an extra special treat (see Tempering, page 34).

❖ Be very careful not to burn yourself, beacuse the boiling mixture is very hot. Proceed with caution and use commonsense, but by all means, do proceed.

❖ Always use a scrupulously clean and dry pan when doing sugar work.

❖ The Turkish delight will absorb the confectioners' sugar, so if you are making these as gifts, be lavish when dusting on the confectioners' sugar-cornstarch mixture, and put extra in the box.

Crème Brûlée

Henry maintains that you can gauge the quality of any restaurant by one mouthful of its crème brûlée. Yet, it's not particularly hard to make well, and is terrifically impressive when you do. This—together with its swoonsome creaminess—makes it a perfect Valentine's Day dessert. We recommend the addition of heart-shape ramekins and Karma Sutra doilies.

Serves: 4	2½ cups **heavy cream**
(you can save two for the next day)	1 **vanilla bean**
Preparation time: 20 minutes	6 free-range **egg yolks**
Cooking time: 30 minutes	½ cup **superfine sugar**
WF GF V	

1. Heat the oven to 300°F. Have ready 4 heart-shape or standard small ramekins.

2. Pour the cream into a saucepan. Cut the vanilla bean in half lengthwise and scrape the seeds into the cream, also adding the empty bean.

3. Heat to just below boiling point, then remove from the heat and let the vanilla steep for 10 minutes before discarding the empty bean.

4. Meanwhile, beat together the egg yolks with ¼ cup of sugar until the mixture is pale and thick. Add the steeped cream. Stir well before pouring into the ramekins.

5. Place the ramekins in a deep roasting pan. Fill the pan with water to come about halfway up the sides of the ramekins, then cover the pan tightly with aluminum foil and bake in the oven for 20 minutes, or until the custard is set but still wobbly. Remove from the oven and let the custards cool without the foil covering.

6. To make the brûléed top, sprinkle a tablespoon of sugar over each dessert (do them one at a time) and, using a blowtorch or a very hot broiler, heat the sugar until burned. Let the burned sugar shell set for 5 minutes before serving.

TIPS

❖ We are opposed to the fashionable habit of adding berries to crème brûlée. It interferes with the pure creaminess of the dish. However, if you must make variations, there are a few interesting flavors that work well:
- Indian: Steep 4 crushed cardamom pods in the custard instead of vanilla.
- Boozy: Add a tot of rum or brandy to the custard.
- Orange: Steep a couple of teaspoons of orange zest in the cream, with, or without, the vanilla bean.
- Thanksgiving: Add a little pumpkin puree and nutmeg. It works. Not on Valentine's Day, please.

❖ These can all be done up until step 6 in advance to save you time. The custard can be made the day before and chilled overnight. You can bake the custard in the morning, then pull the ramekins out of the refrigerator at the end of dinner, brûlée them, and send them straight to the table.

Leon's 5th Birthday Cake

This cake looks crazy—like a gigantic, delicious powder puff, or a Bounty bar turned inside out. It tastes amazing, too. The coconut filling has the texture and flavor of very, very fresh coconut flesh.

Serves: 12–15
Preparation time: 40 minutes
Cooking time: 50 minutes

V

1 stick **unsalted butter**, very soft
1 cup **superfine sugar**
3 free-range **eggs**
½ teaspoon **salt**
2⅓ cups **all-purpose flour** with 3½ teaspoons **baking powder**
¾ cup **coconut milk**

For the syrup
⅔ cup **coconut milk**
½ cup **sugar**
½ teaspoon **vanilla extract**
a pinch of **salt**

For the filling
½ cup **coconut milk**
¼ cup **caster sugar**
¼ cup **water**
1 tablespoon **cornstarch**, mixed with 2 tablespoons **water**
a pinch of **salt**

To decorate
1¼ cups **cream**, whipped
1 cup **unsweetened dry flaked coconut**

1. Heat the oven to 325°F with the fan on. Butter a 9 inch cake pan and line with parchment paper.

2. Cream the butter and sugar until almost white and fluffy. Add the eggs and salt and mix until fully incorporated.

3. Add half the flour until just combined. Add the coconut milk and mix until combined. Then add the remaining flour and mix well.

4. Pour the mixture into the cake pan and smooth the top. Bake in the oven for 40–50 minutes, until a toothpick inserted comes out clean and the cake springs back to the touch. Let the cake cool completely in the pan.

5. To make the filling, put the coconut milk, sugar and water into a heavy saucepan and place over medium heat. Stir to dissolve the sugar and then turn up the heat to high. Add the cornstarch mixture to the pan with the salt and beat until thick. Pour the mixture into a bowl and press plastic wrap over the surface. Let it cool, then chill in the refrigerator for at least 2 hours.

6. To make the syrup, heat all the syrup ingredients together in a small saucepan and cook over medium heat for 5 minutes.

7. Slice the cooled cake into 3 layers. Drizzle with the syrup and sandwich with the coconut filling. Cover the top and sides of the cake with whipped cream and sprinkle with generous amounts of flaked coconut.

BIRTHDAYS

This is a cake that we make at Violet every week. People go wild for the coconut filling, which is adapted from an old Hawaiian dessert recipe. When Henry asked me to create a cake for Leon's fifth birthday this was the first cake I thought of. It just has this outrageous look to it that screams celebration. Plus, it was big enough to feed 350. (If you are tempted to make the Leon version from the photo above, simply multiply the quantities by 30. You will need wooden dowels to support the sheer weight of cake on the top.)

CLAIRE

Triple Chocolate Fantasy Cake

Honeycomb toffee, chocolate, and a hint of apricot make this a dreamy birthday treat.

Serves: 12–15
Preparation time: 25 minutes
Cooking time: 1 hour

Claire developed this recipe for Leon as an extravagant indulgence to add to our cake line-up. During the recipe development we had a meeting with a landlord about a potential site that we wanted dearly. Claire baked a cake for us to take to the meeting (as a bribe). It worked, and in Leon we now talk about our ABC for successful meetings – Always Bring Cake.

HENRY

For the sponge
1 cup **vegetable oil**
2 cups firmly packed **light brown sugar**
1½ teaspoons **vanilla extract**
3 free-range **eggs**
½ cup **plain yogurt**
1 cup **unsweetened cocoa powder**
½ cup **boiling water**
2¼ cups **all-purpose flour**
1½ teaspoons **baking soda**
½ teaspoon **salt**

For the frosting
1¾ sticks **unsalted butter**, softened
1⅔ cups **confectioners' sugar**
4–5 tablespoons boiling **water**
1 teaspoon **vanilla extract**
1¼ cups **unsweetened cocoa powder**

To finish
¼ cup **apricot jam**
honeycomb toffee, crumbled (see page 220)
edible glitter

1. Preheat the oven to 325°F. Grease two 9 inch cake pans and line them with parchment paper.

2. Beat together the oil, sugar, and vanilla. Add the eggs, one at a time, mixing well after each addition.

3. Add the yogurt and mix well.

4. In a small bowl, beat together the cocoa powder and boiling water until smooth

5. Scrape the cocoa paste into the egg mixture and combine into a smooth batter.

6. Sift together the flour, baking soda and salt, and beat into the cake mixture just until incorporated.

7. Pour equal amounts into the cake pans and bake in the oven for 55–60 minutes, or until a toothpick inserted in the center comes out clean. Let cool in the pans.

8. Now make the frosting. Beat the butter until fluffy, then gradually beat in the confectioners' sugar. Add the boiling water and vanilla extract and beat for 3 minutes.

9. Add the cocoa powder and beat until fluffy.

10. To assemble, slice the cakes into 2 layers. Place the bottom layer on a serving plate and spread it with some of the apricot jam. Cover with a tablespoon of chocolate frosting and follow with another layer of sponge. Repeat with the remaining layers, then frost the top and sides with the remaining frosting. Decorate with crumbled honeycomb toffee and edible glitter.

TIPS

❖ For extra decadence, add honeycomb toffee between the layers.

❖ Use the chocolate frosting right away for the best results. It will become firm as it sits, making it more difficult to work with.

❖ Edible glitter can be found online and in many specialty cake decorating stores.

A BAKER WE LOVE

PETRA LEWIS

They say that, before you marry a woman, you should pay close attention to her mother—since that's how she's likely to turn out. I married Mima in the hope that she might, one day, pull something out of the oven to match one of Petra's cakes.

Petra Lewis is one of those unsung "amateur" cooks who puts most professionals to shame. She can make anything, but her particular gift is for the old-fashion cake or dessert. Her kitchen is always full of nostalgic men of a certain age (her husband among them, it should be said), drooling in anticipation of a gently wobbling junket, a vast suet pudding oozing golden lava, or a tower of warm pancakes ready to be slathered in syrup.

All twinkly eyes and silvery hair—like Mrs. Pepperpot but not so shrunken—Petra has the perfect character for cakemaking. As well as being generous to the point of lunacy, she has a patient, meticulous brain. She actually seems to enjoy sitting at her kitchen table for hours pulling the tiny stems off a pound of currants. Some might call it madness; I call it genius.

HENRY

Petra's Christening Cake

Petra makes a christening cake by icing her Fruit Cake (see page 90) with Royal Icing (see page 179). She is a great cake baker, but a nervous icer. Instead of aiming for smooth perfection, she ices this cake pretty roughly and then covers it with ribbons and a menagerie of little creatures bought from sewing departments. The more—and the madder—the merrier.

We always wanted to include a section on wakes because they really can be a celebration of life, and because cooking is one of the ways people instinctively show their love and support in difficult times. On the other hand, we were worried that it might seem a bit gloomy. Then, just as we were about to take these recipes out of the book, someone wrote to Claire asking her what to cook for a wake—so we felt we had to put them back in. Here is how we would like to be remembered—over an Irish coffee and some Guinness cake.

Irish Coffee

Smooth and creamy, a proper Irish coffee is deeply warming and sinfully delicious.

Serves: 4
Preparation time: 15 minutes
Cooking time: none
WF GF V

freshly brewed hot **coffee** (enough for 4)
4 teaspoons **brown sugar**
½ cup **Irish whiskey**
1 cup **heavy cream**, very lightly whipped
4 **Irish coffee glass mugs**

1. Make a fresh pot of coffee.

2. Place a teaspoon of brown sugar in the bottom of each Irish coffee mug and then pour in the hot coffee, leaving about 1 inch room at the top of the mug. Stir gently.

3. Add 2 tablespoons of Irish whiskey to each mug.

4. Pour the barely whipped cream over the back of a spoon and into the mug.

TIPS

✤ The sugar and alcohol both help to float the cream on top, creating the look of a pint of Guinness, so do not omit them.

✤ The idea is that you sip the Irish coffee slowly through the cream, so it is important that the cream is not too stiff.

Guinness Malt Cake

A very moist and rich cake that marries the flavors of a good stout with malt and dark molasses. The dash of cocoa powder adds to the beautiful color. This cake will keep well for up to a week.

Serves: 8
Preparation time: 15 minutes
Cooking time: approx. 1 hour 30 minutes

1 cup **Guinness** or other **stout beer**
2¼ sticks **unsalted butter**
1 tablespoon **molasses**
1 cup firmly packed **dark brown sugar**
1 cup **unsweetened cocoa powder**
2 tablespoons **powdered malt** (such as Ovaltine)
2 **free-range eggs**
⅔ cup **plain yogurt**
2¼ cups **all-purpose flour**
2 teaspoons **baking soda**
1 cup **superfine sugar**
a pinch of **sea salt**

For the stout and cream cheese frosting
½ cup **Guinness** or other **stout beer**
4 tablespoons **unsalted butter**, softened
½ cup **cream cheese**, softened
½ teaspoon **vanilla extract**
2½ cups **confectioners' sugar**, sifted

1. Preheat the oven to 325°F. Butter a 9 inch loaf pan and line it with parchment paper.

2. Place the Guinness, butter, molasses, and brown sugar in a small saucepan and melt over medium heat.

3. Beat in the cocoa and malt, then remove from the heat.

4. In a large bowl, beat together the eggs and yogurt, then add the stout mixture.

5. Sift together the remaining dry ingredients into the bowl and beat all together to combine. Pour into the prepared pan and bake in the oven for about an hour and 15 minutes, or until a toothpick inserted into the center comes out clean. Cool the cake completely in the pan.

6. While the cake is cooling, make the frosting: put the Guinness in a small saucepan and bring to the boil. Boil for about 10–15 minutes, or until the beer has reduced by half its volume. Pour into a container and put it into the refrigerator to cool down.

7. In a mixing bowl, beat the soft butter until creamy and light. Add the cream cheese and beat until smooth. Add the vanilla and the sifted confectioners' sugar and beat well. Now add the cooled, reduced Guinness and beat until creamy and light. Turn the cake out of its pan and spread the frosting on top.

Leon Salted Caramel Banana Split

We introduced this to the Leon menu after extensive—and very sticky—consultations with the under-tens. Madly theatrical and over-the-top, they have proved a hit with diners of every age.

Serves: 6 (with room to spare)
Preparation time: 10 minutes
Cooking time: 10 minutes
WF GF V

1 cup **organic slivered almonds**

2 tablespoons **organic confectioners' sugar**

6 **bananas**

2 cups **organic heavy cream**

½ cup **organic superfine sugar**

sea salt

1 cup good-quality **strawberry ice cream**

1 cup good-quality **vanilla ice cream**

1oz **organic semisweet chocolate**

1. Heat the almonds in a nonstick skillet with the conectioners' sugar until they turn golden and the sugar has caramelized. Put into a bowl and set aside.

2. Slice the bananas in half lengthwise and lay two halves on each plate.

3. Beat 1½ cups of the cream until it is thick. Put it into a pastry bag (a squirty can could save time here).

4. Heat the superfine sugar in a saucepan until it has melted and caramelized—not too dark. Add the remaining ½ cup of cream and stir well. It will froth right up. Heat through to make sure all the sugar has melted into the cream, stirring occasionally. Add a good pinch of sea salt.

5. Put a scoop of each ice cream onto each split banana.

6. Drizzle the ice cream with the caramel. Pipe on the cream. Sprinkle on the caramelized nuts. Grate over some dark chocolate. Serve.

TIPS

For the truly classic split, top each ball of ice cream with a candied cherry.

We sometimes use a runny strawberry compote alongside the caramel as a second sauce.

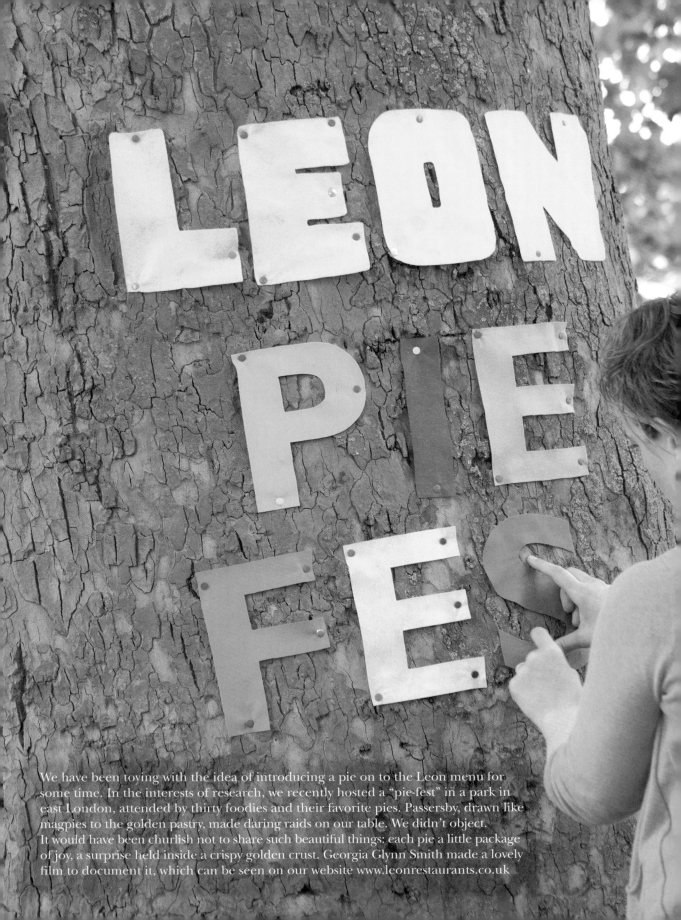

LEON PIE FES

We have been toying with the idea of introducing a pie on to the Leon menu for some time. In the interests of research, we recently hosted a "pie-fest" in a park in east London, attended by thirty foodies and their favorite pies. Passersby, drawn like magpies to the golden pastry, made daring raids on our table. We didn't object. It would have been churlish not to share such beautiful things: each pie a little package of joy, a surprise held inside a crispy golden crust. Georgia Glynn Smith made a lovely film to document it, which can be seen on our website www.leonrestaurants.co.uk

Andi's Marshmallow-Topped Sweet Potato Pie

Serves: 6–8
Preparation time: 35 minutes
Cooking time: 20 minutes
V

13oz **ready-to-bake pastry dough**

4 **sweet potatoes**

6 large spoons of **honey**, or **agave nectar,** or any sweetener that you prefer

1 teaspoon **ground nutmeg**

1 teaspoon **ground cinnamon**

1 teaspoon **ground allspice**

1 teaspoon **vanilla extract**

2 tablespoons **dry flaked coconut** (optional)

3 **free-range egg whites**

1 package of **white mini marshmallows**

1. Preheat the oven to 350°F.

2. Roll out the dough big enough to line a 10–11 inch fluted tart pan. Bake blind for about 25 minutes, until the pastry is golden. Remove from the oven and set aside to cool, keeping the oven on.

3. Peel the sweet potatoes and cut them into cubes. Boil until soft, then mash them well.

4. Put the sweet potatoes into a large bowl with the honey, nutmeg, cinnamon, allspice, vanilla extract, and the coconut (if using). Mix thoroughly.

5. Beat the egg whites well in a separate bowl, then add to the sweet potatoes and whip the mixture together for a few minutes. Pour into the pastry shell and bake in the already warm oven for about 20 minutes.

6. When the top of the pie has a few browned peaks, it is ready to come out of the oven. Gently arrange the marshmallows on top in any design that you like.

7. When you are ready to eat the pie, place it under a hot broiler to toast the marshmallows, which will turn golden and start to melt very quickly. Keep a close eye on it so that they don't burn.

ANDI AND HER BROTHER SEAN, 1969

283

Esther's Pork Pie

Makes: 1 large pork pie
Preparation: 2 hours
Cooking time: 1¾ hours

ESTHER IN OXFORD, 1989

3 tablespoons **butter**, diced

¼ cup diced **lard**

½ cup **water**

2¼ cups **all-purpose flour**

¾ teaspoon **salt**

1 free-range **egg**, beaten, plus extra **beaten egg** for brushing

1lb **pork shoulder** or **leg**

4oz **pork belly**

4oz **bacon**

salt, pepper, thyme, mace, chili, or any other seasoning you like

¼ cup **powdered beef gelatin**

1. Heat the butter, lard, and water in a saucepan until it is melted and warm, but don't let it boil. While the fat is melting, put the flour and salt into a mixing bowl and make a well in the center. Pour the egg into the well and half mix it in with a knife. Once the fat and water have melted together, add to the flour and mix until it forms a dough.

2. The dough will probably be a bit too sticky, so sprinkle on more flour until it takes on the glossy sheen of dough. Form it into a ball, wrap it in plastic wrap and chill in the refrigerator for an hour.

3. When you take it out of the refrigerator you can cut off a quarter to put aside for the lid—but I find that if you are using a pie mold (8 inches in diameter and 6 inches deep) it's easier to roll out the whole batch, lay it over and press it into the mold, then cut off the excess and reroll that to make the lid.

4. Don't be afraid to make the walls of the pie really thick—up to ½ inch or more. The crust is just a vessel for the pork inside; it's going to have to be robust enough to contain hot pork fat AND the warm jellied stock you are going to pour in later. If it's a dainty ¼ inch thick, it will tear on cooking.

5. Heat your oven to 350°F. Mince up your pork pieces finely in a food processor. Sort through the meat after it's been processed to pick out any pieces of gristle or rind.

6. Add salt, pepper, thyme, mace, chili or anything else you'd like to the filling. You can test the filling's seasoning by cooking a small piece and tasting.

7. Fill your dough-lined pie mold with the pork filling, really ramming in as much as you can. However much you stuff it, it will all shrink on cooking, so don't be afraid to squash in as much as possible, pummeling it all in, like punching a sleeping bag back into its carry-case.

8. Now roll out your remaining dough to make the pie lid. You must, *must* brush beaten egg around the top edges of the pie to seal the lid to the sides. Nothing else will do: If you use anything else, the lid will come away from the sides and stuff will fall out and it'll just be a disaster.

9. Lay the lid on top of the pie and press it all around the edges to seal. Trim away the excess dough round the sides.

10. On the top of the pie, in the center, make a good, generous hole in the pastry, about the width of your little finger. This is so that juices can escape during cooking and for pouring in the stock at the end.

11. Brush the lid with more beaten egg and shove it in the oven for 30 minutes. Then turn the heat down to 325°F and cook for another 1¼ hours.

12. Let the pie stand in the mold until completely cold— this might take 4 or 5 hours. During cooking, the pork will have shrunk away from the sides of the pastry to form a natural cavity to be filled by the gelatin.

13. You can make the gelatin in two ways: the first of these is to make up 2½ cups of warm beef stock—any sort will do, from a bouillon cube or whatever—and set it with powdered gelatin. The second, if you're feeling very serious, is to ask your butcher for some veal bones or a pig's foot. Boil it for a couple of hours with some carrots and celery and the stock will turn to gelatin when it sets, without needing the help of manufactured gelatin.

14. Pour the gelatin stock through the hole in the top of the pie while the stock is still lukewarm, and it will set around the pork as it cools. This is a tricky process. You can use a turkey baster if you've got one, or a large measuring cup and funnel. Don't lose heart if the stock bubbles out of your pie's blowhole and goes everywhere. This kind of pastry is pretty resilient. You may have to repeat the pouring in of the stock after you've poured in the first batch, because it will slowly disappear into the nooks and crannies of the pie and suddenly there will be a ½ inch gap between the lid of the pie and the top of the gelatin. Chill the pie in the refrigerator for at least an hour before eating.

Hattie's Black Currant Tart Canelle

Serves: 6–8
Preparation time: 25 minutes
Cooking time: 25 minutes
V

HATTIE IN OXFORD, 1978

1⅓ cups **all-purpose flour**
6 tablespoons **unsalted butter**
⅓ cup **superfine sugar**
2 **free-range egg yolks**
1 tablespoon **water**
1 tablespoon **ground cinnamon**
2 cups **black currants**, trimmed
milk or **beaten egg**, to glaze
extra **superfine sugar** to sprinkle over,
    plus more to add to the currants

1. Preheat the oven to 350°F.

2. To make the dough in a food processor, put in the flour, butter, sugar, egg yolks, water and cinnamon and process until it comes together into a ball. Remove from the machine, cover with plastic wrap and chill well for at least an hour in the refrigerator.

3. To make the dough by hand, mix together the flour, butter, sugar and cinnamon with your fingers until you have a bread-crumblike consistency. Slowly add the egg yolks and water until the mixture comes together into a ball. Cover with plastic wrap and chill well.

4. Put the black currants in a sauce pan, cover generously with superfine sugar, and put over low heat. Stir, and when you are sure that all the sugar has melted, turn up the heat until the fruit is bubbling and thick. Remove from the heat.

5. Roll out the dough ½ inch thick and line a 7 inch tart pan, gathering up any trimmings. Fill the tart shell with the black currant compote, and roll out the trimmings to make a thin and neat extra strip to go around the edge. There should be enough dough leftover to make a lattice pattern over the top of the tart if you wish.

6. Brush the dough with milk or beaten egg and bake in the oven for 20–25 minutes, until the pastry is golden. Serve cool, with vanilla ice cream or crème fraîche.

Ana's Cheese Empanadas

Our Ecuadorian cleaner Ana doesn't speak much English, but makes herself understood through the language of laughter, kindness, and exceptionally good empanadas. Great party food.

Makes: 20 small empanadas
Preparation time: 30 minutes +
30 minutes resting time
Cooking time: 10–15 minutes

V

3¼ cups **all-purpose flour**
2 teaspoons **baking powder**
1 teaspoon **salt**
1 stick **butter**
¼ cup **orange juice**
⅓ cup **sparkling water**
8oz **mozzarella cheese**
1 medium **onion** grated or finely chopped
1½–2 tablespoons **superfine sugar**
1 **free-range egg**, lightly beaten
extra **caster sugar** to sprinkle on top (optional)
vegetable oil, for frying (optional)

ANA, IN EQUADOR, AGED 11 YEARS OLD

1. Put the flour, baking powder, and salt into a food processor and process until mixed.

2. Add the butter, orange juice, and sparkling water and process until a dough forms.

3. Put the dough onto a surface, bring it together into a ball, wrap it in plastic wrap and place in the refrigerator for 30 minutes to rest.

4. Grate the mozzarella into a bowl and add the onion. Add the sugar and mix well.

5. Preheat the oven to 400°F. Line a baking sheet with parchment paper, or oil it well.

6. When the dough has rested, remove it from the plastic wrap and dust your work surface with flour. Cut the ball of dough in half (it's easier to roll out smaller amounts). Roll out the dough so that it's about ⅛ inch thick.

7. Using a 3½–4 inch cutter, cut circles out of the dough. Place a teaspoon of the cheese filling in the center of each circle, fold the dough over to make a half-moon shape, and seal the discs, pressing down with a fork. Make sure they are all well sealed, otherwise the filling will ooze out when you cook them.

8. Brush the empanadas with the beaten egg, and sprinkle a little sugar over the top of each one if you want that extra sweetness. Place on the baking sheet and cook in the oven for 10–15 minutes, until golden. Cool on a wire rack.

9. If you prefer the fried option, fill a saucepan 1–1½ inches deep with vegetable oil. When the oil is hot, deep-fry the empanadas until golden, and sprinkle with superfine sugar before serving.

Janet's London Fields Apricot & Cherry Galette

Serves 6–8
Preparation time: 30 minutes
Cooking time: 45–50 minutes
V

JANET IN NORTHUMBERLAND, 1978

For the pastry dough

1 cup **all-purpose flour**, plus extra for dusting
a pinch of **salt**
a pinch of **sugar**
6 tablespoons cold **unsalted butter**, cut into ½ inch pieces
¼ cup **ice-cold water**

For the galette

10 fresh **apricots**, washed and halved, pits removed
1⅔ cups **fresh cherries**, washed and halved, pits removed
2 tablespoons **sugar**
1 tablespoon **all-purpose flour**
1 tablespoon **almond meal** (optional)
1 **free-range egg**, beaten

1. Combine the flour, salt, and sugar in a bowl and either cut in the cold butter with the back of a fork or use two knives.

2. Avoid overmixing—leaving larger chunks of butter than you would expect will make the pastry more flaky. Drizzle in the water and bring it all together into a ball without working the dough. Wrap in plastic wrap, then flatten into a disk and let it rest in the refrigerator for about 45 minutes.

3. Heat the oven to 400°F and line a baking sheet with parchment paper. Let the dough to come to room temperature so its easier to work.

4. Dust a work surface with flour and roll out the dough into a circle the size of a dinner plate. Put it on the baking sheet and return it to the refrigerator for a few minutes.

5. Remove the dough circle from the refrigerator and sprinkle the sugar, flour, and almond meal over, leaving a 2 inch border around the outside. Arrange the fruit on top of the almonds—you can put the cherries in the middle and the apricots in circles around them, or make up your own pattern.

6. Fold over the dough rim to create a crust. Brush the rim with beaten egg, and bake in the bottom half of the oven for 45–50 minutes, until the fruit is squashy.

7. When cooked, transfer the galette onto a wire rack to cool.

8. Serve warm or cold, with vanilla ice cream or whipped cream. Or simply enjoy it on its own with a cup of coffee.

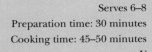

TIPS

This is basically a free-form, open-face tart and it can be used for all different kinds of fruit.

LONDON W1F 7JE
LEON.
35-36 Gt. MARLBOROUGH St.
Fair Trade & Organic
NOME DEL
PASSEGGERO
BAGAGLIAIO

FRESH LEON-MADE
LEON
LEMONADE

MOROCCAN
MEAT BALLS
MOROCCAN HERBS & SPICES   PLUM TOMATO SAUCE
1 2 3 4 5 6 7 8 9 10 11 12 S

LEON-HOTEL
CASABLANCA

LEON

GRILLED CHICKEN
SUPERFOOD SALAD
1 2 3 4 5 6 7 8 9 10 11 12 S

MAGIC MACKEREL
LEON
COUSCOUS

POWER
SMOOTHIE
LEON

LEON
FRESHLY-SQUEEZED
ORANGE JUICE
LEON

LEON   LDN

LEON   LDN

LEON

London Fields Apricot and cherry galette by Janet

Maggie's Croatian Pear Pie

This pie can be done in a square, oval or any shape pan you prefer. Also, the pears can be cut into halves, quarters, or slices, depending on the look you like.

Serves: 4–6
Preparation time: 50 minutes
Cooking time: approx. 45 minutes

Maggie was our son George's nanny for the first three years of his life, and is still a great friend. A former judo champion, she has buns of steel and incredible natural authority. One of the reasons children love her – apart from the fact that she can swing them round her head one-handed without breaking a sweat – is that she's a wonderful cook, thanks in part to the tutelage of her Italian–Croatian parents. This is a typically elegant dish.

HENRY

4–6 ripe **pears**

For the pastry dough
1¼ cups **superfine sugar**
1 stick **unsalted butter**
3 cups **all-purpose flour**
1 **free-range egg**
¼ teaspoon **baking powder**
a pinch of **salt**

For the almond filling
1¾ sticks **unsalted butter**, softened
1⅔ cups **confectioners' sugar**
2 free-range **eggs**
2 free-range **egg yolks**
a dash of **Calvados** (optional), or other alcohol
2 cups **almond meal**
½ cup **all-purpose flour**

For the glaze
⅓ cup **apricot preserve**

1. Heat the oven to 425°F.

2. To make the pastry dough, mix together the sugar and butter until you have a smooth paste. Add the remaining ingredients to the bowl and mix together well, adding a little water if you need to. The dough will be very crumbly, but do not despair—it's supposed to be like that.

3. Roll out the dough and line a 10 inch tart pan, pricking it all over with a fork. If the dough is too crumbly, press it into the pan by hand a little at a time. It should make a thick crust of pastry, so don't be alarmed by the amount you have. Line it with parchment paper and fill with pie weights. Bake for 8–10 minutes, depending on your oven, then remove the paper and weights and let cool.

4. Peel the pears, leaving the stems on. Cut them into slices or halve them, removing the core carefully so they don't break.

5. To make the almond filling, cream together the butter and sugar, then add the eggs and egg yolks, one at a time, mixing after each addition. You can do this by hand or using an electric handheld mixer. Add the alcohol if you are using it, then the almond meal, and flour, and mix well.

6. Pour the filling into the pastry shell, and assemble the pears on top, in any which way you like.

7. Bake the pie in the oven for 30–40 minutes, or until golden brown, but do not let it burn. Let cool in the tin.

8. Heat the apricot preserve in a small saucepan with a teaspoon or two of water until it is runny and spreadable, and while still warm, use a pastry brush to glaze your pie.

TIPS

✦ Eat this pie lukewarm on its own, with cream, or a good vanilla ice cream.

✦ To make this in a loaf pan, bake for another 20 minutes on a low oven shelf.

Henry's Spiced Chicken Mystery Pie

The mystery is that no one can believe it's made with rhubarb. The pink stems are wonderful in savory dishes, adding body and a subtle citrus flavor. Worth trying in lamb stews, too.

Serves: 4–6
Preparation time: 10 minutes + cooling time
Cooking time: 2 hours 45 minutes

1 large **chicken**

olive oil

salt and freshly ground **black pepper**

6 **rhubarb stems**, cut into 1 inch pieces

2 **bay leaves**

4 **cardamom pods**, crushed with the back of a knife

1 glass of **white wine**

2 **white onions**, peeled and sliced vertically into 8 wedges

1 tablespoon **turmeric**

1¼ cups **heavy cream**

12oz ready-to-bake **puff pastry** (or 1 x quantity Flaky Pastry Dough, see page 38)

1 **free-range egg**, to glaze

1. Preheat the oven to 350°F.

2. Rub the chicken all over with olive oil and plenty of salt and pepper.

3. Put all the ingredients, except the cream, pastry, and egg, into a casserole dish. Put the lid on and place in the oven for 1½ –2 hours. The chicken should be falling off the bone. (Check now and then and add a dash of water if it seems dry.)

4. Let the chicken rest until cool enough to handle. Pick off the meat and put it into a pie plate with the vegetables and juice from the casserole, discarding only the skin, bones, and bay leaves. Stir in the cream. Season. You can now put this into the refrigerator until you want to make the pie (several days later, if you prefer).

5. When the filling has cooled completely and you are ready to cook the pie, heat the oven to 325°F. Roll out the pastry dough to make the lid, and use the trimmings to cut out a decoration for the top. I like to write the word "Pie". Glaze with the beaten egg.

6. Cook the pie for 40 minutes or until the top is golden.

Claire's Cherry Pie

Sour cherries are a favorite pie filling in this country. Sour cherries grow in Great Britain in many back yards because the bright red fruit is pretty. They don't survive well going to the supermarket. In either country, if you can't find them fresh whether from a friend's tree or your local farmers' market, frozen ones can be used. A last resort would be cans of preserved ones, but make sure to drain off most of the liquid first.

Serves 8
Preparation time: 40 minutes
Cooking time: 1 hour
V

1 x quantity **Flaky Pastry Dough** (see recipe on page 38)

3 cups fresh or 2 cups frozen pitted **sour cherries**, preferably Morello

1 cup **superfine sugar**

¼ cup **cornstarch**

a pinch of **salt**

1 **free-range egg**, for brushing

a little **milk**

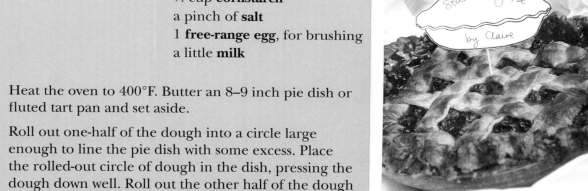

1. Heat the oven to 400°F. Butter an 8–9 inch pie dish or fluted tart pan and set aside.

2. Roll out one-half of the dough into a circle large enough to line the pie dish with some excess. Place the rolled-out circle of dough in the dish, pressing the dough down well. Roll out the other half of the dough into a rectangle ⅛ inch thick and place it on a baking sheet lined with parchment paper. Place both in the refrigerator while you prepare the filling.

3. Put the cherries, sugar, and cornstarch into a bowl and add the salt. Toss to coat the fruit evenly.

4. Remove the pie dish from the refrigerator and fill it with the cherry mixture. Remove the rectangle of dough from the refrigerator and use a small knife to slice the dough into ¾ inch strips. Arrange the strips of dough over the cherries in a lattice pattern, saving 3 strips for the edge.

5. Crack the egg into a small bowl and add a few drops of milk. Beat to combine. Trim the edge of the dough to the rim of the dish. Using a pastry brush, carefully coat the lattice with egg wash. Use the last 3 strips to cover the rim, then brush this with the egg wash as well.

6. Place the pie in the oven for about an hour, with a piece of aluminum foil underneath to catch any drips. The pie is ready when you see the fruit filling bubbling through.

RECIPE INDEX

INDEX

a platter of figs and other recipes

THE NATIONAL TRUST

Traditional Puddings

Sara Paston-Williams

IVER CAFE COOK BOOK   Rose Gray and Ruth Rogers

ULGE   100 PERFECT DESSERTS
CLAIRE CLARK
LE CLERC   LITTLE CAKES

The Anatomy of
DESSERT
With a Few Notes on Wine

EDWARD A. BUNYARD
Introduction by
MICHAEL POLLAN
Preface by
DAVID KARP
MODERN LIBRARY FOOD · RUTH REICHL, SERIES EDITOR

TART
BRE

BY CHAD ROBERTSON
PHOTOGRAPHS BY ERIC WOLFINGER

EZ PANISSE FRUIT   ALICE WATE

DAVID
LEBOVITZ   RIPE for DESS
100 OUTSTANDING DESSERTS WITH FRUIT   INSIDE OUTS

MARTHA STEWART'S PIES&TARTS

PRUEITT/ROBERTSON   TARTINE

«IN THE GREEN KITCHEN»   ALIC

BABYCAKES   Vegan, (Mostly) Gluten-Free, and (Mostly) Sugar-Free
Recipes from New York's Most Talked-About Bakery

Smith's   Book of Cakes

Jane Grigson's   Fruit Book

Darina Allen's
BALLYMALOE COOKERY COURSE

The Art of

A year in my kitchen   SKYE GYNGELL

l Slater

II   BEYOND NOSE TO TAIL

FERGUS H
JUSTIN PI

THANK YOU

From Henry:
Claire, who has a rare talent for baking and an even rarer one for having fun. What a joy to have you as a neighbor • Mum for being the original inspiration and for continuing to inspire me to cook • My wife, Mima, for proofing, reproofing, reassurance, rewriting, ideas and even the odd leg rub • Everyone at Conran; in particular, Jonathan, Sybella, and the wise owl Lorraine • John for his continued support and for providing a little AC current now and then • Dad for getting it and unflinching support • Liza and Kate, my sisters, for all your useful thoughts about Leon • Georgia and Anita for putting up with the chaos and producing such beautiful things out of it • Jeremy, for all those hyphens • All of the Leon managers for their extraordinary passsion • Simon Drysdale - to mix a metaphor, a rock in the eye of the storm - without whom everything would grind to a halt • Tom Ward for your perseverance and moral compass • Justin Ovenden for the outstanding fridge displays and general hutzpah • Steve and Agnieszka for making it all add up • James Lee French - what did we do without you • Glenn for an amazing future. What a difference you have made • Benny O for your love of narrative • Georgie Sanderson - for caring so much and understanding Leon inside out • Belinda Giles for the pig days, the board days, and the investment • Benny and Rich - good luck to you • Bruno Loubet for setting me on my way • Nick Evans, who had no idea what he was getting himself into • Xander and Hannah Armstrong for having such faith in the world's worst godfather • Giles, Mark, Simon and the unflinching workers at the Sustainable Restaurant Association • Petra for being a baker I love • Roly and Susan Chambers for coming and going but always being around • Bambi Sloane • Charlie Bigham for the meatballs • All of the people who have invested in us • Craig from Barton and White • Rick, Sophie and Kate and the Fusion gang • Jo, Laura and the Saucettes • Greg - we love you really • JD - for reigniting the fire occasionally • Andy, Glenys and Mel for being so generous with your children • Pierre and Kathleen Condou - for endless support • Linda Fox - a truly wonderful person. One day we'll come to the States. • Stan and Tony and everyone at Reynolds • Adam Longworth for the Ganeshes • Allegra - we'll get there for you • Tim Smalley for navigational advice in tricky waters • Jacques Fragis for ferocious focus • Spencer Skinner • Gavyn Davies • James and Hannah Horler - thanks for Toph • Giles Coren and the way he fights the cynics in the battle for sustainability • Jason Lowe for the amazing photos on our menu boards • All of those who gave recipes to the book • All of the recipe testers for making sure the recipes were easy to understand • All of those who baked wonderful pies at the pie fest, but which didn't make it into the book •

From Claire:
Henry for creating a fantastic new way to eat good food fast. For being such an ardent supporter of my business, Violet, and for inviting me to do this terrific project with him • Hattie Deards for being so jolly in the face of two totally overcommitted authors • Lorraine for support and confidence • Georgia and Anita for total dedication and enthusiasm • Kate McCullough and Echo Hopkins for being great assistants, above and beyond • Special thanks to Dri and the Violet girls for keeping the shop and stall running so well • Thanks to Sam for the great studio at The Shop on Haliford Street • Thanks to Sara Tildesley for teaching me so so much • Finally, thanks to Damian for that ring!

From Anita:
Felicity MacDonald Bing for enthusiasm and support on the shoots • Sam at The Shop for his patience and cake eating abilities • Matilda Harrison, Sonja Bucherer and Lucinda Cooper for additional props • Lisa, for help with those kids • Matt, Maddie and Cy Pie for everything else.

THANK YOU

To all Leon family members, past and present: Ben Peverelli • Marta Klosinska • Peter Kancian • Malgorzata Herda • Ildiko Tanacs • Nicola Bartsch • Agnieszka Chmieliauskas • Justin Ovenden • Navina Senivassen • Ursula Bowerman • Guilherme Turibio Da Silva • Simon Drysdale • Thomas Ward • Remigijus Chmieliauskas • Justyna Konca • Anna Sobczak • Maciej Marek • Piotr Jablonski • Stephen Oakley • Sini Marika Mulari • Kadija Begum • Agata Cyminska • Rodrigo Menezes De Carvalho • Kristal Maley • Thomas Green • Lucy Buckingham • Igor Kurosu • May Kovacova • Rute Christina Coelho da Rocha • Deivid Grigorid • Marta Kowalska • Rachel Little • Bozena Bobowska • Liliya Georgieva • Bruno Lupi • Richard Holmes • Suzanne Carter • Isabela Santos • Ben Iredale • Liang Sun • Jaroslaw Zybowski • Tahsin Kucuk • Orlan Masilu • Jenny Russell • Renan Amorin • Nicolas Bracamonte • Mara Casolari • Roberta Rimkute • Stephen Bage • Lucy Harrison • Holly Clare • Ashleigh Davewport • Jirina Kralova • Christine Noel • Katre Kurosu • Yok Ming Chung • Grace Kyne-lilley • Efemena Okogba • Matthias Abdul-Haiat • Danilo Oliveira • Katrina Hassan • Natalia Koc • Robert Beaney • Gary Marriott • Matthew Ali • Laura Silova • Lara Wrubel • Jenna Brehme • Shipon Miah • Vasilica Cirican • Penny Munn • Ryan Yates • Alexia Farina • Vadims Belovs • Megan Bailey • Monika Jaworska • Pedro Barchin • Thomas Davies • Patricia Ferreira Martins • Saga Levin • Elisabeta Gjovani • Viktor Kanasz • Claire Didier • Ravi Kondru • Oxana Popa • Shaun Ryan • Michaela Boor • Anna Kempi • Christopher Ali • Nuria Olmedo Nieto • Anita Moser • Alessandro Bononi • Karolina Driessen • Joshua Parker • Caio Skua Nagao • Juan Lopez • Pedro Ribeiro • Matthew Alp • James-Lee French • Jean Carlos • Carlos De Oliviera • Shaun Oxenham • Anastasija Nigul • Anderson Gomcalves • Mara Locisano • Joshua Martins • Ilaria Frigerio • Mariana Gontijo Pizeli • Jurgita Lukaseviciute • Bernardo La Porta Da Silva • Maria Laranjeira • Marta Goszczynska • Gentil Silva • Jessica Wratten • Erika Leonaviciute • Rajiv Jaligana • Istvan Szep • Egle Narbutaite • Chanell Scott • Justyna Stanislawa Jesiolowska • Elodie Kouame • Mark Prove • Martyn Trigg • Olga Chwilowicz • Miguel Gonzalez Alonso • Owen Myers • Biodun Adetimehin • Gytis Sirinskas • Jurgita Sirvinskiene • Francisco Luis Gom Silva • Ramos Barbosa • Judith-Ryanatu Gbadamassi • Gustavo Burkle • Naomi Clare Mullins • David Ncube • Denzso Zrinszki • Modesta Peckatyte • Trevor Payne • Vladimirs Gutans • Pedro Simas • Ilona Staniuk • Janis Viksne • Reda El Guebli • Nora Ivette Goboly • Bernando Aragao • Steph Brown • Samuele Raiano • Dan Kenna • Manuela Eller • Didier Bussillet • Giada Zerbo • Alvaro Santamaria • Ineta Bliudziute • Melanie Cunnane • Marcos De Souza • Luca Gennati • Nora Szosznyak • Luis Javier Diaz Moreira • Sandra Navaro • Talita Heshimi • Dominika Staniuk • Matthew Atkinson • Letisha Dyke • Daniele Arcangeli • Toni Kapeli • Silje Graffer • Celine Pelzak • Hector Martin Alonso • Georgina Sanderson • Benjamin Oliver • Monika Mieszczak • Viera Varvaruova • Amita Shrestha • Marisa Batistussi • Janos Szima • Simona Cijunskyte • Henrietta Okai • Elvyra Rekusce • Valentina Manea • Micheline Essomba • Fabio De Micheli • Artur Jakubowski • Anna Marczenko • Yoel Tewolde • Pawel Bojanowski • Amy Browne • Leigha Vigilant-Thomas • Joao Veterano • Egle Ozolaite • Catia Rodrigues • Lacey Lawfon • John Corrigan • Georgina Roper • Remmond Theophilus Johnston • Lukasz Przytarski • Patricia Perez Violan • Susanna Alessandroni • Paloma Solbiati • Kayleigh Goodger • Maxine Haher • Elzbieta Paslawska • Marcelino Vaccaro • Desiree Haley • Sachelle Macgregor • Nicolle Dawkins • Fernando Lopez • Viktoria Marianna Raj • Alejandro Garcia Jinorio • Joseph Balog • Marco Bernardi • Mark Sorsky • Nerijus Latakas • Rodrigo Muniz • Kamila Webb • Eimear White • Donard Marshall • Miriam Poveda Abad • Anna Anuscenko • Vydmante Kalvynaite • Raquel Peralta • Anna Rodero Carro • Thomas Malley • Nicola Kibble • Alessandro Vioto • Ysbrand Iodice • Isis Sitbon • Alan Gullo • Raffaele Coletta • Nina Amaniampong • Jessica Merrett • Julian Gomes • Heider Resende Das Neves • Thomas Malley • Mohamed Ouali • Arnaud Jouin • Kelly Agbo • Guoda Jankunaite • Wilson Inga Orega • Angela Aloy • Antonio Carlos Dos Santos • Lucas Zanca • Matthew Sears • Veronika Prokesova • Nicoline Lyck Bech • Amber Petersen • Janos Francis • Katrina Bulman • Vanessa Mazzi • Anneish Dwyer • Enara Lekanda • Lauren Hounsell • Sebastian Clark • Simone Badiali • Karlie-Sian Meagre • Adriana De Oliveira Viega • Jay Ricketts • Gina Smith • Andew Sabapathy • Franlesco Sponza • Birgit Arumetsa • Dean Leacey • Innocenzo Colacicco • Pablo Sanchez Ruiz • Detroit Williams • Nilton Caboco • Emma Louise Stevens • Rossanna O'Mahoney-Lamb • Nathan Joshua Gordon • Medhi Abdel Haiat

Dedications:
To my sons George and Johnny—able trenchermen. And to my wife, Mima, who makes everyone around her feel they have so much to give. — HD

For Damian and Shuggie. — CP

First published in 2011 by Conran Octopus Limited,
a part of Octopus Publishing Group,
Endeavour House, 189 Shaftesbury Avenue, London WC2H 8JY UK
www.octopusbooks.co.uk

An Hachette UK Company
www.hachette.co.uk

First published in US in 2012 and distributed by Hachette Book Group USA,
237 Park Avenue, New York, NY 10017 USA

Distributed in Canada by Canadian Manda Group
165 Dufferin Street, Toronto, Ontario, Canada M6K 3H6

Text copyright © Leon Restaurants Ltd 2011
Design and layout copyright © Conran Octopus Ltd 2011
Illustrations copyright © Anita Mangan 2011 (except cake on cover and
page 39 © Matilda Harrison 2011)
Special photography copyright © Georgia Glynn Smith 2011

Publisher: Lorraine Dickey
Managing Editor: Sybella Stephens
Project Manager: Hattie Deards
Design and Art Direction (for Leon): Anita Mangan
Art Director (for Conran Octopus): Jonathan Christie
Illustrations: Anita Mangan (except cake on cover and page 39 by Matilda Harrison)
Special Photography: Georgia Glynn Smith
Production Manager: Katherine Hockley

ISBN 978 1 84091 611 9
Printed in China

Jossy, David, Kate, Joseph, Kay,
Ed, Nicholas, Jane, & Henry, August 1977

Marion and John, 1973

Jonathan and Johnny, 2011

Claire

Henry's birthday, Putney, London 1977

Soli in Dubai, 1989

John and the gang

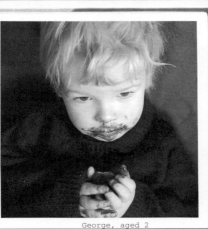

George, aged 2

Claire, 1978

Anita's birthday, 1974

John at Broadstairs, aged 3

Liza and Henry, 1977